The journal of a Buddhist mortician

COFFINMAN

The journal of a Buddhist mortician

COFFINMAN

BY SHINMON AOKI

Translated by Wayne Yokoyama

BUDDHIST EDUCATION CENTER

Originally published in Japanese as *Nokanfu nikki*
©1993, 1996 Shinmon Aoki

Buddhist Education Center,
909 South Dale Avenue, Anaheim, CA 92804

Copyright ©2002 Buddhist Education Center
and Wayne S. Yokoyama
All Rights Reserved Published 2002
Printed in the United States of America
2002107361

Cover and book design by Arlene Kato
Calligraphy by Reverend Akio Miyaji
Cover photo: ZEFA/Photonica

ISBN 0-9721395-0-8

CONTENTS

FOREWORD

This little book, a diary of a mortician, invites the reader into the fascinating world of Buddhist spirituality which sees the extraordinary in things ordinary, mundane, and even repugnant. Written with deep affection for life and poetic sensibility, the author Shinmon Aoki evokes the world of boundless compassion found in Shin Buddhism which evolved from the Pure Land tradition of Mahayana Buddhism in thirteenth-century Japan.

Coffinman is not a standard English word but a translation of the Japanese, *nokanfu*, whose job was to pick up a corpse, place it in a coffin, and ultimately prepare it for a funeral. The author, a failed businessman and once aspiring writer, is a coffinman, which invites nothing but rebuke from family and friends. But he conveys a refreshing view of life that only a person in his position can bring.

Once when he emptied a bucket of water, used for washing a corpse, near the trunk of a bamboo, he sees the translucent body of a dragonfly filled with eggs and observes:

> Just a short time ago as I was doing the coffining
> surrounded by people crying, no tears came, but
> when I saw eggs shining in the dragonfly, tears
> filled my eyes.....
> The tiny dragonfly dying after a few weeks
> has been bearing eggs in unbroken succession
> to perpetuate its life form from hundreds of
> millions of years past.

The author sees life in death, or Life/Death in Buddhist discourse, manifested in the luminous face of the dying. When he goes to the hospital reluctantly to visit his uncle who had cut off all ties with him with disdain and even anger, he writes, "That face of his was so soft and gentle, it virtually glowed. The next morning my uncle died." It is this glow that Coffinman sees everywhere in life, especially "in the faces of many of the deceased, the glimmering faces of that radiant light floating about." Once when picking up a corpse left untouched for several days, he notices maggots and says, "A maggot is just another life form. And just when I was thinking that, I was sure I saw one of them glow with light."

This light is none other than Inconceivable Light (*amitabha*), one of the many synonyms for Amida Buddha. Amida is not a being who emits rays of light but a radical awakening of the numinous. According to the author,

This Inconceivable Light is immeasurable, reaching
everywhere without limit. It penetrates all things
and has neither shape nor form. It exists in eternity.
If we think of it as a light that comes to us from
eternity, then it's constantly near us, constantly
shining upon us.

Inconceivable suggests that this light is beyond conceptual
understanding but not beyond experiential awareness.
Aoki explains, "In that moment when Life and Death suddenly integrate, that Inconceivable Light passes before our
eyes like a shooting star."

This is reminiscent of the advice that Basho once gave to
his students on the craft of haiku poetry: "Capture in words
the passing moment radiating with light before it vanishes
from sight." Religiously speaking, this passing moment radiating with light is captured in the Name, *namu-amida-butsu*.
In the intoning of the Name, the Inconceivable Light that
is *amida-butsu* penetrates through each finite, limited
namu-being, making possible the liberation from all
karmic bondages.

This light is also the radiance in the countenance of
Shakyamuni Buddha as he is about to preach *The Larger
Sutra of Infinite Life*. Just as Kasyapa's smile marks the leg-
endary beginning of Zen, so likewise Ananda's praise of the
Buddha—filled with serenity, radiance, majesty and lofty
resplendence—marks the beginning of Pure Land Buddhism:

Deep in the state of Great Serenity
The Buddha's radiant face was wondrous to behold,
As Ananda astutely observed,
Winning him praise from the Buddha
For inquiring as to the matter.

This radiance was also experienced by Shinran, the founder of Shin Buddhism, who spent his ninety years on earth to make it accessible to all beings. Countless are the people who have received this luminosity through his teachings contained in the *Tannisho* ("Grievous Differences") and his major opus, *Kyogyoshinsho* ("Teaching, Practice, Faith, Realization"). Among them, Aoki the coffinman, with "eyes like the clear blue sky and transparent like the wind," shares this rich spiritual legacy with quiet humor, penetrating insight, and boundless compassion.

BY TAITETSU UNNO

PREFACE

Zen is a very well known term that is used throughout popular Western culture. In fact Zen is so well known in the West that many do not even realize that it is a school of Japanese Buddhism. Shin Buddhism is another school of Japanese Buddhism. In Japan, Zen Buddhism and Shin Buddhism are the two largest Buddhist schools with Shin Buddhism actually being the larger. However, Shin Buddhism is not nearly as well known and has lagged far behind Zen Buddhism in being able to penetrate the consciousness of the Western mind. This book is intended to reach beyond the traditional Shin Buddhist community in hopes that the Western world can become more familiar with the depth found in Shin Buddhism.

Therefore, the editors of *Coffinman* have tried to make this book appeal to as wide an audience as possible while still being true to the intent of both the author and the translator. We tried to remove any phrases or colloquialisms that were uniquely Japanese and would be lost on those outside of the tradition. However, we did maintain many of the original Japanese terms when no appropriate English analog existed. Translating a perfectly good Japanese term into a misleading English one is something we tried to avoid.

This points out another difficulty. English is a very direct and dualistic language, while Japanese has many subtle nuances. In English, it is very easy to state facts in black and white. This makes English the preferred language for both law and science. But English does not communicate as well in areas such as emotion or spirituality, which are inherently ambiguous. These subjects tend to be very gray and are hard to quantify. For example, in English one cannot find too many words that describe the continuum of feelings between the words love and hate. This adds to the difficulty when editing a book in English that was originally written in Japanese.

There are also cultural differences between East and West. The Western mind tends to explain concepts using deductive reasoning. For example, in the West one would first state the conclusion, "I am going to prove D." From there, he would show how A implies B, B implies C, and C implies D. In the East, the conclusion is not overtly stated. In the example above, one would instead talk alternately about A, B, and C. All the while, trying to get the reader to intuit D. Some use the derogatory term circumlocution. I prefer to think of this as a moth circling the flame rather than as talking in circles. The effect of this writing style is quite powerful if one can remain open to whatever will come.

Coffinman is not an academic or intellectual work. This is why we decided not to use footnotes. We found footnotes to be very distracting. Instead, we have provided a section of notes at the back of the book. The notes are very extensive and can be thought of as a fourth chapter. It may be beneficial to read or at least review the notes prior to beginning the book. The background provided by the notes will help make this book much more accessible. The entries in the notes are words, phrases, and titles found in the book. They are listed in alphabetical order along with the page number of the first occurrence of each entry. The first occurrence of the entry is also marked with a diamond (◊) in the text.

We struggled with the issue of name order. In Asia, it is customary to list the family name first and given name last, but this can be very confusing for the Western reader. Initially, we tried using the traditional Asian name order but had trouble dealing with names like D.T. Suzuki and Issa. We did not want to use Suzuki D.T., and Issa is so famous that he is known worldwide by only his first name. It is also difficult for a Western reader to detect the name order being used when the names are so unfamiliar. For example, it is easy to discern with names like Smith John but not so easy for names like Kaneko Misuzu. We also wanted it to be easy for readers new to Buddhism to look up names on the Internet and at bookstores and libraries. It would be sad indeed if one gave up a search simply because he was looking up the first name instead of the last. We mean no disrespect, but for these reasons we chose the Western name order of given name first and family name last.

Another issue that is as delicate as name order is that of gender. We had hoped to make this book gender neutral by changing half the examples in the book from references of "he" to "she," but it is very hard to maintain consistency with this simplistic approach. We also tried changing all the references from "he" to "they" but then we had problems with subject-verb agreement. For example, "He walks." and "They walk." Next, we tried changing "he" to "one", but this has a far too formal sound. We also did not want to use "he/she" so we decided that we would ignore the issue of gender. We learned that this is a common problem when one writes in English and that we were not going to solve it with this book.

When making edits we tried very hard to do no harm. We only made edits if we felt they would clearly make the book better. If the change would only make it different, then we did not make the change. For example, we stayed away from any changes that were merely a matter of style. Style is the province of the author and the translator, not of the editor.

We wish to sincerely thank the author Shinmon Aoki for recording his very personal spiritual journey. His story captures the essence of Shin Buddhism. He wrote from the heart and not from the mind. We would also like to thank the translator Wayne Yokoyama for bringing this work to the Western world. We would also like to acknowledge Reverend Taira Sato, who first brought *Coffinman* to Wayne Yokoyma's attention and suggested that he translate it into English, and Professor Yoichi Kaji of Otani University in Kyoto, for editing an early draft of the English translation. Not enough books written on Japanese Buddhism have been translated into English.

Dr. Taitetsu Unno, the author of *River of Fire, River of Water*, also made a major contribution to *Coffinman*. Dr. Unno proofread the draft and made many corrections and suggestions. He also edited and rewrote many of the notes. We also felt very honored when he agreed to write the Foreword. More importantly, he helped resolve some very subtle doctrinal issues as only he could.

I would also like to thank the editors of *Coffinman*: Sandi Clendenon, Arlene Kato, Cliff Uejio, and Ronnie Young. These individuals worked many long, hard hours, and it was their enthusiasm that convinced those around them that this book would be published. We would also like to thank Reverend Marvin Harada. It was Reverend Harada who first suggested that we publish this book. Not only was he instrumental with all Buddhist doctrinal questions, but he also used every meeting as an opportunity for additional dharma talks. I think many of us participated as editors in order to spend more time learning Buddhism from Reverend Harada.

Along with the editing of the book we had the job of the actual production and publication of the book. Arlene Kato did a wonderful job designing the cover art and formatting the book. Reverend Akio Miyaji graciously supplied the calligraphy, and Gilbert Nishimura provided all the necessary legal services pro bono.

Lastly, we would like to thank both the Sangha and the Board of the Orange County Buddhist Church for giving us the opportunity and the resources to take on such a project. Many members of the Orange County Buddhist Church helped proofread and made corrections on the initial drafts of *Coffinman*. This improved the quality of the book immensely. Editors tend to become so close to the work that they cannot see the most obvious mistakes.

Of course, in the end we are all responsible for this book. This includes the reader. We thank you most of all for taking the time to read *Coffinman*.

Namuamidabutsu

JON TURNER

Chapter 1

THE SEASON OF SLEET

"The sleet's lonely as can be.
I stand precariously
On two blocks of granite,
Where the two elements of snow
and water come together,
This branch of glistening pine is
Covered with snow drops
of ice-cold water—this
I receive this—the last thing my
gentle little sister will ever have."

Woke up this morning to the sight of Mt. Tateyama covered with snow. I was feeling tingly all over. My new job starts today, washing corpses and coffining them. It made me nervous just thinking about it, and I wanted to back out, except I'd already gone and told everybody a few days ago. Finally, I decided, *hell, I'll just do it.*

There's more to washing corpses than meets the eye. It's not just bathing them. You've got to wipe them down with alcohol, put them in their white "Buddha-robes," fix their hair and faces, put their hands together with an *ojuzu*◊—all of this in preparation for coffining.

Just my luck my first customer was a hefty fellow. Once a carpenter, this old man of seventy years was weaving his way home on his bicycle after a night out drinking when he tumbled into a gutter and died. I'd had plenty of chances to watch other people wash and coffin corpses. That was part of the training for this line of work. But I sure had a heck of a time doing it myself and soon found myself sweating like a pig. The arms of the corpse were so stiff I couldn't get them through the sleeves of the Buddha-robes. And unless you held on to the corpse from behind, you couldn't tie the straps around the waist. There I was in action, with two or three dozen family members and next of kin watching me with bated breath.

The first time I held a corpse I had to banish from my mind the fear of death, the revulsion of dead bodies. Throwing myself into the task, I worked frantically, frenzied, fighting off waves of nausea, completing it heaven knows how. On top of that, just as I was about to leave, all of the bereaved family members got up and, with hands placed together and speaking in respectful tones, came all the way to the entrance to see me off, even though the sutra chanting for the wake had just begun. It was altogether strange. Got home and switched on the bath myself. All the while my wife was peering at me with an odd expression.

In this part of the country, it's the custom even today that the washing and coffining of the deceased be done by the men folk, that is, cousins or uncles or nephews. The two or three men selected would come trudging along reluctantly, having been appointed to the task by the town council or village elders or the funeral home. For some reason they always show

up in the weirdest outfits—old aprons and cooking smocks
turned inside out, with belts braided out of rough rope
cinched tightly around the waist. And just when they are all
set to begin, they each take a long slug of whisky to brace
themselves. Which is the last thing they need, really, since
they're already so jittery they can't do anything right. As the
coffining progresses they each take turns being in charge, boss-
ing each other around every time some little thing goes wrong.

The custom of scrubbing down the corpse is to make
the body as clean as possible for the final send-off. This is
especially true for someone who's been bedridden for a long
time; after all, it's the least we can do for them. These days,
with the number of hospital deaths on the rise, the method of
washing has switched to using alcohol to wipe the body. But
here in this part of the country, when a person dies at home,
the old custom prevails. The corpse is immersed in a tub of
cold water topped off with hot water and then scrubbed clean.

Besides having too many people running the show, these
amateurs faced with this rather unnerving task are half
drunk out of their minds. Stripping the corpse naked, first
they sit the body up and then they lay the body on its side.
This causes the blood to ooze from the mouth and nose
and ears, making the corpse a foul and bloody mess. In the
meantime, our unfortunate gentlemen waffle between
feelings of fondness and affection for the deceased and fear
and loathing of the corpse, with their feelings of revulsion

only aggravating their already agitated state even more.

Today, I was the one confused. It never occurred to me there were still places that buried their dead sitting up. This was a small hamlet on the outskirts of Toyama◊ where they said no one had died for the past four or five years. And despite the fact that a new crematorium serving the entire city had just been built here, they still were inclined to practice the old village custom of sitting burial for which they had their own special facility equipped with a funeral pyre.

Everything was going fine washing the corpse and putting the Buddha robes on. Then we got to the part where the corpse had to be positioned to sit in the coffin. Here I was stumped. As I was shuffling around looking uncertain, an old man who must have been a village elder came up to me and said, "What's the matter, sonny, ain't never done a sitter before?" and proceeded to help out. With ropes and long strips of white cloth on hand, the old man began to fold the legs into a position where they could be tied to the torso. It was hard to bend the legs, and we couldn't get them in the right position for the coffin until the old man bound them so tightly they made a popping sound.

Well, that ought to do it, I thought. But then the old man gathered up all the remaining strips of white cloth and started to wrap them round the corpse again and again. I heard he did this to make sure the spirit of the deceased would be locked in tight and wouldn't get out. But just awhile ago,

when the body was recumbent, we secured a small sword to its breast for protection. They said this was done to keep the evil spirits out. I got all confused by this. Anyway, there were a lot of things in this business of last rites I couldn't quite make heads or tails of.

After that, there were no more requests for washings and coffinings for a while, but it seems there has been a sudden rush of orders lately. Whenever someone calls about a funeral, our receptionist always starts off by saying, "Well, if it's coffining service you need, leave it to us. We've got a great man for that on our staff."

We were swamped with orders today. We had calls from three different locations, and it was almost ten o'clock at night by the time I got to the third house. Night had fallen on the village, but I could spot the house of the bereaved right off. In the darkness with all its lights on, the house stood out like a road sign. In front of it, five or six people were standing on the dirt road. When I got closer, they all started complaining to me. The ceremony for the wake was already delayed two hours, and the priest was obliged to wait for three hours in the meantime. That's why everyone was so edgy. The colleague my company had sent to arrange the altar was being held hostage. I had to go in and apologize profusely, touching my head to the tatami mat. When the coffining was finished, the deceased was laid out at the altar, and a sigh of relief passed over the faces of everyone present when the sutra chanting for the wake finally began.

My colleague who had been held hostage told me that the priest who was forced to wait gradually became irritable and demanded that the relatives of the deceased do the coffining themselves. The relatives looked at each other and fell silent. The host kept saying over and over again they were waiting for the coffinman; he's going to arrive soon.

And so that's how I got the name Coffinman.

Got home and looked it up in the dictionary. No such word.

The snows came to the Tateyamas, clear sunny days alternating with dark rainy ones for two or three days at a stretch. Winter had set in in the Hokuriku. It was rainy today. Now, due in part to the inclement weather, it becomes dark sooner than usual. The rain starts to get colder and colder by degrees.

One dark evening with cold rain falling, an uncle of mine whom I hadn't seen in over ten years showed up all of a sudden. I had a hunch as to what this was all about the moment I saw him on our doorstep, so I whisked him off to a nearby coffee shop. Just as I'd thought, his gripe with me was simple. "So what makes you think it's OK to do what you're doing, huh?" he asked. Not ten days had passed since I'd taken up my new job, and since it was known only to my wife and some close friends, I wondered how he'd gotten wind of it. Then I realized that a relative of mine must've been among the people calling to express their sympathy at one of the funerals we did.

My uncle started off saying he had a good job lead for me, but in the course of the conversation he let me know that as the eldest son from our ancestral home that goes back generation after generation, I had no business becoming a coffinman, and that I was a complete damned embarrassment to the whole family. Was I not aware that we boast amongst our relatives, educators, law officers and government employees, and that this gives us a certain amount of prestige in society? And then he added as a final touch that unless I quit my present job they would cut off all ties with me.

He left after I promised to find some way to leave the company. But in my heart I had already grown obstinate. There was no need for him to remind me of what my relatives did — that I knew quite well. Ever since I had been old enough to think for myself, it had been drummed into me that I had certain responsibilities as the eldest son from the ancestral home. That burden hung around my neck and dragged me down into a pit of failure and despair time and time again. Even then my uncle had the gall to threaten me by saying he'd cut off all ties; this was what my relatives had already done to me long ago.

Besides, I thought to myself, what's all the fuss about? Doctors and nurses and members of the police criminal iden-tification section must handle corpses like this all the time. Is that any better than what a coffinman does? After I'd calmed down a bit and thought about it, I realized this line of work goes beyond what's socially acceptable. For there's nothing lower on the social scale than the mortician, and the truth of the matter is that we fear the coffinman and the cremator just as much as death and the corpse. It seems the line of work I chose violates some basic taboos. When I realized this, it made me feel uneasy.

But why was it I chose this line of work in the first place? I certainly had no answer for it when my uncle put the question to me. I may not have been sure exactly why I took up this line of work. But one thing was certain: the choice I made was not entirely by my own will alone. Looking back now, I feel as if I had been destined to take the path I did by some unseen power guiding my life.

I was four when my parents took me to Manchuria. I was eight when World War II ended. My sister and brother who were born in Manchuria in a refugee camp died while awaiting repatriation. I thought my mother had died of typhoid fever, and I clearly remember I was taken care of by an unknown lady who went with me to the place where the corpses were piled up to dump the bodies of my sister and brother. In October 1946, I was repatriated along with my mother, who had somehow managed to survive. Father had been sent to the Siberian front, never to be heard from again.

When I returned to the house where I was born in Toyama, my grandfather and grandmother were living on the premises

of a spacious old-style estate. This was one of the large farms
that once dotted the alluvial plain where the Kurobe River
spills out from the mountains. The village was made up of
more than fifty households scattered on broad and spacious
fields. Of these, about half had the same family name as ours.
Ours was the main one, the ancestral home from which all
others branched off. It was a household that had been around
for generations, until the Agricultural Reforms left us with no
way to support ourselves.

It never occurred to my grandparents to work by physical
toil, and in the end they were reduced to selling what was
stored in their private storehouses. And so they kept up their
elegant lifestyle, even though there was nothing in the larder
for tomorrow. Mom got on so poorly with Grandpa that she
once fled to Manchuria because of it. And so after a brief
sojourn home, she left the house to work in the Toyama black
market. I passed my boyhood on the estate. When it came
time to go to college, Grandpa sold the last of the storehouses
and part of the estate to make up the money for the college
entrance fee. It was then that the ancestral home that had been
handed down for twenty-eight generations collapsed forever.

When I entered college in Tokyo, the campus was being
swept by the storms of protest against the 1960 U.S.-Japan
Security Treaty, and all the lectures were cancelled. I was an
indignant young man who soon found himself participating
in student demonstrations. The Security Treaty went into

effect, and everything seemed to grind to a halt. Just then, I got an urgent telegram saying my mother was seriously ill, and so I returned to Toyama. As it turned out, mother's illness, appendicitis, had been misdiagnosed, and she soon got better. In the meantime, I started helping out at a bar she was running and got so involved there I never returned to college.

After a while, I wanted to have my own place, so I opened a cafe-style pub. In those days, I was writing poetry, and my shop became a hangout for poets and artists. I ran the joint enjoying a drink with the customers. It became well known locally for its unusual atmosphere and so was prospering.

One day the novelist Akira Yoshimura walked in out of the blue. There I was in my role somewhere between bartender and customer. When I mentioned I wrote poetry, he asked if I'd ever written a novel. He told me that if I ever did a short story to let him know. And then he was gone. That was all. In the meantime, the wine and the women began to take their toll on me, and while it was great hanging out with the poets and artists, the shop was starting to do badly. Well, if you go into this kind of work with no business sense and fool around while working, what do you expect?

One day I remembered what Akira Yoshimura had said to me, and I started to write a short story. It was about my grandfather who had no income during the ten-year postwar period but spent all of his time looking after the persimmon grove in the courtyard of our estate. I sent the manuscript to

Yoshimura and was told it would be published in the literary journal *The Writer*. Later, he sent me a copy of the journal with the piece I did called "The Flames of Persimmon."◊ With it was a note saying I was invited to attend the meeting where they'd review this issue among themselves.

Before I went to the meeting, I had absolutely no idea that *The Writer* was formed around a literary coterie headed by Fumio Niwa and made up of a number of prominent writers. After the meeting, I followed Yoshimura to a round of bars in Shinjuku and even followed him home. The next morning when I awoke at the Yoshimura residence, there was his wife, Akutagawa award winning writer, Setsuko Tsumura, fixing breakfast for us. At the table they both encouraged me, saying, "You have the stuff, so keep those novels coming."

With that one compliment, I felt like a country hog that had shinnied up a tree. I put all thoughts of managing the shop out of my mind and sat down to a stack of manuscript paper. Even if I hadn't done that, the shop was already on the verge of bankruptcy, and it was only a matter of time before it folded. The only thing left was a pile of debts. But even as it was going under, that country hog who shinnied up a tree kept his nose buried in manuscript paper.

In the midst of the confusion of bankruptcy, when we were scraping the bottom of the barrel for the last of our small change, my wife gave birth to our first son. We were so strapped for cash that we couldn't even buy formula. If only I could sell a novel, then we could buy all the formula we needed, I told her. But I was only spouting off, and what I said only made me feel hollow.

Then one day, when my wife and I were having a big argument, she threw the newspaper in my face and my eye happened to fall upon an announcement in the want ads. It said: "For ceremonies to start a new life. Help wanted." I didn't know what kind of job it was, but I went for an interview anyway. When I walked into the entryway, there was a stack of coffins on the side. I thought, "Damn, what am I getting myself into?" But I needed the job to buy the formula, and so I plucked up my courage and got myself hired by the company.

This morning on my way to work I raised my eyes to the sight of the snowcapped Tateyamas. Oh, how beautiful they were, even to a coffinman. I had no coffinings scheduled for today, so I headed for the crematorium where I had been told some time ago to pay a call.

The crematorium was located on the southernmost edge of Toyama city. As I drove from city center, the front window of my car was filled with a panoramic view of the Tateyama mountain range, and after thirty minutes in that direction all signs of human habitation vanished.

Arriving at the crematorium's row of ten furnaces, I was shown around the back, an area usually restricted to official personnel. It seemed like the work for today was over, as I could see only three or four staff members cleaning up.

I was standing there looking around when all of a sudden a man with round, black spectacles appeared. He put a small tea tray down on a table covered with a light film of ash and waved at me to take a seat. Then the man with the round, black spectacles and a short chubby man sat down on either side of me, hemming me in. Both of them were grinning like bears.

Their beef with me, they said, was that they were having trouble recently with someone putting stuff inside the coffins, and that someone was me. We can't allow you to comply with the family's wishes to put something the deceased was fond of inside the coffin, they told me, leaning over toward me *yakuza* style.

I was just about to protest that these coffins come from all over the city, and it's not necessarily the case that I did the work. But the big grins on their faces were still there. I decided not to say anything more since it seemed they knew clearly which funeral parlor was conducting which services and who did the coffining.

You're the one who put the rugby ball in the other day; weren't you, they said. Well, OK, I did remember doing something like that. It's true we just did a coffining two days ago for a teacher who was the coach of the rugby team for many years. And the fact is, one of his former students did ask if it'd be all right to put a rugby ball in, and I said it would.

The short guy pointed to the man with the black spectacles

and told me that he had a glass eye on the right because, in the days of the old furnaces, when he was checking the kiln through the peephole, something blew up inside and a fragment shot out, piercing his eye.

In years past, when the coffin arrived, the practice was to have the mourners take leave of it at the lobby, after which it would be wheeled around back so that its contents could be examined before it was put in the kiln. But then someone sent a letter to the newspaper saying they saw a crematorium employee searching around the body as if pilfering something. Ever since then the policy has been to put the casket into the kiln from the lobby-side where everyone can see.

Because of the nature of the work they do, the crematorium workers felt they were being made fools of. They talked at length, telling their side, getting more and more excited as they did. Actually, it was someone who suspected them from the first that made the insinuations, saying that there was a gold tooth or ring missing that ought to have been there.

They insisted that, as for those gold teeth and rings, with the kind of oil burners we use for the kilns these days it gets so hot inside, they just vaporize into nothing. There's not a trace left of them. Although I don't really think it gets so hot that they do that.

They kept blathering on like this, flecks of foam leaping from their mouths. At first I couldn't tell whether they wanted to complain or to give me a sermon. The gist of their spiel was that their line of work is hard and demanding, and people don't appreciate the pains they go through. They are nominally "city employees," but in society they are the object of ridicule, with people calling them names like "the spooks who cremate the dead." And for all the crap they had to take, their pay was low.

The big thing they wanted to impress upon me was that for the past two or three years the amount of gratuity has been fixed and not increased. And this was the fault of the morticians, whose advice had caused this problem. Originally the amount of gratuity depended on how generous the paying party was, and, they said, it was strange to have a set amount decided beforehand. The morticians were the ones who set the fee scale for the mourners, in effect setting an upper limit on what could be paid.

The conversation was so one-sided I thought I'd chip in a few words. "And so the gratuity amounted to more than your regular salaries."

"Damn fool, you don't know jack. There were five of us before, and now we've added one more. But the amount of gratuity has stayed the same, is what I'm telling you."

After I'd been called a damned fool, the conversation sort of stopped. Anyway, what they talked about went off in all directions, but it always came back to the problem of money. "Since you're a coffinman we think you ought to understand. If you thought this work didn't pay well, you wouldn't be in it in the first place. You must be making a killing yourself." And they fixed me with a serious look.

After promising them I'd never again put anything dangerous in the coffin, I excused myself. When I stepped out of the front, the crematorium buildings were thinly veiled in darkness, and a magnificent sunset was forming in the clear blue sky. As if something were beckoning to me, I drove toward the embankment road of the Joganji River which flowed along the back of the crematorium. From atop the embankment there was an unbroken view of the Toyama plains fanning out, a scene that this unruly river helped carve out.

As the late autumn sun began to set in the distance over the Kureha Hills, a pale evening glow spread across the entire sky. In the eastern sky, the ridgeline of the snow-capped Japanese Northern Alps was outlined in red. Driving along the river enjoying this magnificent spectacle, I noticed a red dragonfly flying ahead of me just beyond the front window. Then, looking more carefully, from the clumps of gumi trees that dotted the riverbed I saw thousands upon thousands of red dragonflies flying toward the plains. A full third of them were locked in copulation while in flight. After spending the summer months in the Midagahara Meadows, the dragonflies all return at the same time. Changing from dull brown to brilliant red, they take flight into the magnificent sunset.

If you think about it, from the past beyond all reckoning, the dragonfly has been flying into the sunset, even before humankind made its appearance. In this one moment of autumn afternoon, as they take to the sky, they perpetuate the life of their species that's been preserved for millions of years. It's as if their brilliant red color comes from having been immersed in all these countless sunsets.

An approaching car passed me, and I decided to head back. Against the black surface of the river, boats with fishermen on board looked like shadow picture silhouettes. The salmon were running. The salmon too, in this one moment of autumn, were traveling upstream, fully believing in the eternal cycle of life.

For all living things, late autumn in the north country is a time to prepare for winter, a time to perpetuate their life forms. It's a busy season for all.

After a lull in business, some work washing and coffining finally came in.

Although I didn't notice anything when I got the rough map to today's house, I stopped dead in my tracks at the entrance. Why, this is the house of the girl I'd been seeing when I first came back to Toyama from Tokyo! Ten years had passed since I had seen her.

Her eyes were like clear limpid pools. We often went to concerts and art exhibitions together. Her old man was strict and always wanted her home by ten o'clock, and many a time I dropped her off in front of this house. Once when we were saying goodbye, I tried to kiss her in the car, but she said she wanted me to meet her father first, so I told her we'd get around to that some other time. After that I don't know how many times she asked me to meet her father, but our relationship ended before that ever happened. But we didn't part on bad terms.

I had heard through the grapevine she'd gotten married to someone in Yokohama. As I walked through the door, I kept telling myself she probably hadn't come back yet. Glancing around the room I couldn't see her. And so with a feeling of relief, I started the washing.

By now I had done so many cases that anyone watching how deftly I moved would surely see me as a pro at work. But there I was sweating profusely, the same as the first time, and this had come on as soon as I had the corpse and begun to work. The sweat on my brow was about to run down, and just when I was about to wipe my forehead with the sleeve of my white robe, there she was, reaching out to wipe my brow — how long she'd been sitting there I don't know. Tears welled up in those beautiful eyes. She sat next to me until the work was finished, mopping the sweat from my face.

As I was taking my leave, the family representative, who seemed to be her younger brother, knelt on the tatami mat and politely bowed and expressed his thanks. Behind him I could see her standing there just like that, her eyes filled with so many things that needed to be said but would never come to pass. Even after I got into my car, I couldn't get the memory of her eyes — brimming with tears yet touched with surprise — out of my mind.

How she had pleaded with me to meet her father. No doubt she had loved her father dearly, and her father had loved her. And in the midst of her sorrow, the surprise of seeing me washing his corpse was understandably a bit much. But deep within the surprised look in her eyes there was something more. Even her sitting by me to wipe the sweat away, all the way through the procedure, was a gesture of no ordinary dimensions. And she did this right in front of her husband and relatives. I felt there was something there that transcended the trivial world of scorn or pity or sympathy, that even went beyond the relationship between man and woman.

I felt that she showed me she accepted my total existence just as I was, no more no less. And so thinking I began to feel good about myself. And I began to feel I could continue in this line of work.

Work is work, and one kind of work is just as good as any other. But though we think so, the reality is that the mortician and the cremator will always be abominated as long as death is seen as taboo.

There was a time when people in show business were looked down upon, but now they are the talk of the town. Once, in the feudal society of warrior, peasant, craftsman and merchant classes, the merchants occupied the bottommost rung. Now, the world of big business leads the government around by the nose. Even if our overall situation doesn't improve much, there must be some way for our profession to at least not be the object of ridicule in the eyes of society. The business of conducting funeral rites may change in the future, but will no doubt continue to be provided in some form or other, as long as there are people around. If that's the case, then something has to be done.

It's strange to think that our own fathers and mothers, who on an ordinary day would have loathed associating with such people, were the recipients of their kindness at the end of their lives. In ages past, the priestly profession, respected for their role in helping others, was intimately involved with conducting funeral rites. Today this earns them the derogatory name "funeral priests."

When you brood on these matters, it only makes you depressed. It didn't bother me so much when my uncle bad-mouthed me, calling me a disgrace to the family. It was when my friends started to drift away that it really got to me. It was tough going bankrupt. Friends bailed out on me like tiny spiderlings scrambling out of the egg. On top of that, when they heard I was now washing corpses for a living, it's not hard to guess why they suddenly turned cool toward me. But more than that, it was how people looked at me that did it. It made me wary of them, and I started to avoid meeting people. The more I worried about it, the smaller and more insignificant I felt. I lost all desire to write that novel, and all the pages I'd done up to then ended up in the trash.

That something I perceived deep within those lovely eyes filled with sorrow and surprise resolved everything for me. So, from that day on, everything changed. Once it happens, you realize there's nothing simpler than the workings of the human heart. You go about with a chip on your shoulder, begrudging society for what should have happened to you but didn't—all of this is to blame someone else for your situation. Then you realize there's someone out there who accepts you just as you are and that alone restores you to life. How you regard yourself changes completely. While I would comment on the social taboo on death, I didn't realize that I myself was an extension of it. If I wanted to effect a change in that convention, all I had to change was my own way of thinking. Change a person's thinking and that person changes what he does.

I immediately went to a medical supplies store to get myself a surgical robe, mask, and thin rubber gloves that doctors use during an operation. Changing into uniform and not forgetting my best manners, I went to my next coffinings earnestly and brimming with confidence. I had come into my own as Coffinman.

Stepping onto the scene like this had a noticeable effect on everyone present. Yesterday, for instance, I had an appointment at a farmer's house in the foothills. The coffining done, I was served some tea, when a lady older than the deceased I had just coffined came scooting up to me and said, with a serious look on her face, "O Doctor sir, when it's my turn to go, you *will* come to do me up, won't you?" Well, being called "Doctor sir" wasn't what I had expected, but it bowled me over when she asked for an appointment. Imagine someone making an advance appointment for a particular coffinman. But I was not put out by her request, and so I said, "I'm sure we can arrange that," an answer that brought a smile to her face.

And today yet another thing happened. After the coffining was done, I was shown to the waiting room the priests use. As I was sharing a spot of tea with the priest, he said, "Damn, I just saw you at work and you were amazing! There's a lot that we can learn from you. But, tell me, which med school did you attend?" The question came so suddenly I didn't know how to answer. Just then our conversation was interrupted as he was called out to finish the arrangements for the wake. I don't know why I had to be from medical school, but one thing was sure: up to now I hadn't projected that image when doing coffinings. Change how you think of yourself and you change the way people perceive you.

My thoughts gradually started to focus in on what it was that people had missed up to now. In the course of work, meeting with the people at the crematorium and the funeral parlor and the priests, I noticed the problem they were up against. While death was always something ever present, they averted their eyes from looking at death.

If you go into your line of work thinking it inferior, as you perform your duties, it shows that you bear within yourself a feeling of inferiority. You try to make up for it by doing it for the money. Do that and you leave behind all hope of ever improving the social standing of your line of work. Do that and you become the reason society looks down on you, the reason you begrudge society your lot. Averting your eyes from the very heart of the work you engage in, there's no way you can come into your own in that role. There's no way others can put their trust in you. As long as you go around thinking there's money to be made from this dirty line of business, whatever the job might be, people around you will always look down on you for it.

There are splendid things you can set down in a journal. You can even convince yourself that what you're doing is right. But don't expect the real world to give you a break.

At some point or another my wife found out the nature of my work. But she didn't let on she knew. She just held it inside, the indignity of it.

Last night, when I went to her seeking affection, she turned me down. "And I won't," she said, "until you quit that disgusting job of yours." I tried to talk some sense into her, but she said, you ought to think of our children's future, and finally she broke down and started to cry.

"Okay, okay, I'll do something soon," I said, trying to wriggle out of it. And I tried to approach her again.

"You're defiled! Keep away from me!" she said hysterically, refusing my advances.

This upset me so much I couldn't sleep. It was especially her calling me "defiled" that got to me. She had refused me once before, saying, "You're defiled! Keep away from me!" But that was when she found out I was having an affair. The words didn't anger me then. In fact, I wasn't bothered at all. But the other night when she screamed, "You're defiled!" the words pierced me like the point of a knife. I sat there stunned.

That words could stun and anger me meant they struck a sore spot in my makeup. You can carry this sore spot around with you every day. It's not until someone tears it open and jumps on it that your blood boils and you flare up. This is especially strong when the words gouge out the abyss of human existence. These are never words of noble sentiment. Rather, they are usually coarse expressions rooted in socially accepted ideas of our ethnic or tribal group, ideas that have become an integral part of our makeup. Just one such word can precipitate an act of murder or even an act of war.

The word "defilement" has been present in Japanese society from ancient times to the present day. Whatever ideas or cultural influences flowed into this island nation from the continent, they could never extirpate this notion deeply embedded in the Japanese mentality. It has survived and has been passed down intact to each succeeding generation. In this sense it's very much like the genetic information encoded within the chromosomes that are rigorously transmitted and of which we are the recipients.

Folklore studies were started in this country by Nobuo Origuchi and Kunio Yanagida. They investigated the folk customs and ceremonies of marriage and funerals in every area of Japan. The conclusion they arrived at was that underlying much of folk culture was this primitive, simplistic belief in defilement and purity.

What was "defiled" is stipulated in fair detail in the ancient work *Rites Extending Good Fortune*. Two of the most important forms were death defilement and blood defilement. Death defilement was understood as the impurity of death or the dead. All things associated with death or the dead were regarded as impure. Blood defilement was the defilement of the loss of blood from a wound. However, blood defilement also meant the defilement of blood loss that women experience at the menses. Women were thus regarded as defiled beings.

Even today some areas of Japan still have an excrement defilement. They call it *owai*. Just as the lavatory is sometimes referred to as the "unclean place," excrement became targeted as another form of defilement.

Ridding oneself of all forms of defilement thus became a major preoccupation of these people. They averted their eyes from it, pushed it as far from themselves as possible, drew a line between it and them, prohibited women from participating in certain sectors of society, and made all kinds of efforts to keep from being defiled.

But there are times we can't distance ourselves from it. At those times ceremonies of exorcism and purification are done to make the unclean and defiled pure once again. These ceremonies turn the defiled into the pure in an instant.

The word pure is associated with a clear day or formal wear worn on pure and solemn occasions. As to the relation of defiled and pure, it's seen in the rule that once the sumo ring is purified it cannot be entered again by a woman. Also, mountainous places like Mount Hiei,◊ Mount Fuji, the Tateyamas, and Hakusan were regarded as holy mountains and were made off limits to women.

When a person dies, the family affixes a slip of paper to the front of the house to announce it is in mourning. When the members of the household return from the crematorium, they ritually cleanse themselves with purification salt. This is also a practice that arises from the notion of defilement and purity.

As to why salt is used in the rites of purification, this is said to go back to a legend in the *Record of Ancient Matters.*◊ When the Shinto◊ god Izanagi◊ returned from the Yomi, the "sulphur springs" land of death, he announced that the Land of the Yellow Springs was a realm of defilement. He then proceeded to purify his body of defilement with sea water. All rites go back to this account in the Record, the seawater now symbolized by the separate elements of salt and water. Down to this day, salt and water have been used continuously in rites of purification for well over a thousand years.

Salt and water are used in the sumo ceremony; salt and the water in the hand-bucket are used in the funeral ceremony; sprinkled water and salt are used in the Japanese eateries. All of these are instances of the ritual tools of salt and water to transform the defiled into the pure. The notion thus lives on, along with other ceremonies for the gods performed in Japanese Shinto. The roots of this belief run deep. It's a problem you can't use logic to explain or resolve.

After my wife said, "You're defiled," I was unable to sleep and passed the night turning the pages of some old books.

<hr>

At last the sleet came. It was as if the autumn leaves on the mountain were being pursued by the falling snow on mountain tops and, to keep a safe distance, had fled to the foothills. The sleet began just as the leaves on the persimmon trees at the farm houses in the foothills started to fall, one or two fruit hanging on the tips of the branches like bright red globes.

As we entered the season when the sleet starts to fall, everywhere in the village the salmon were hung out all at once. Starting from the sushi shop that made *masuzushi*, they were lined up and hung to dry from poles placed horizontally in the row of platanus trees in front of the fish store. With rough rope passed through their gills, their mouths open wide, they stared at the sky with steel eyes.

In the sky above, stormy nimbostratus clouds piled up on the Tateyamas, engaging one another as they sat low astride the ridge, refusing to budge. From the leaden sky the sleet continues to fall with no letup. This cold monochrome landscape sopped with sleet is one of the faces of nature unique to this region. The weather creates the face of the natural world here. It's not that the snow falls on the mountains; rather, the snow works to create the mountains.

When the sleet begins, the people living in the Hokuriku◊ sense the onset of winter. Depending on the year, it can be as early as the last third of November or as late as the last third of December. Thus, we have another season altogether, "the season of sleet," that other areas of Japan do not.

There's no English word for *mizore*. The dictionary gives the word "sleet," an icy cold rain, but mizore is neither rain nor snow. When it comes to ambivalent phenomena like *mizore*, the English language seems to have difficulty coming up with an appropriate term. The English language thus seems to have difficulty with words that express phenomena that fluctuate between points.

The same can be said about the word *shoji*, or "LifeDeath."◊ In Western thought, it's got to be either life or death; there's no way to grasp LifeDeath as a single unit. In this respect, Eastern thought, especially Buddhism, grasps "LifeDeath" as a unit. As far as that goes, the relation of life to death is like the relation of rain to snow in sleet. In the singleness of LifeDeath = sleet, there can be no sleet if the rain is separated out from the snow.

However, just as the ratio of the rain to the snow fluctuates depending on the temperature, the ratio of life to death varies according to time and circumstance. During times of war, for instance, when famine and plague ravage the land, the amount of death is greater than usual. When death is the greater, it's spoken of more often, and death may even be seen as something beautiful. In the present age where life is emphasized, death has no hold on our daily life and thought. Death has lost the battle and tends to be treated as something evil. The tragedy of today's thinking that death is to be abhorred as evil and life accrued absolute value, is the fact that everyone must die one day, bringing us face to face with an absolute contradiction.

Even when we encounter the death of someone close to us, such as a relative or a friend, we may have a passing sentiment of how grateful we were for that person, but we are not made conscious of death on an everyday basis. When someone else dies, it's someone else's death. Someone else's death does not become an occasion for letting it develop into an understanding of what Buddhism calls our interrelatedness. For instance, the passage, "Though in the morning we may have radiant health, in the evening we may be white ashes," from Rennyo's letter on the *White Ashes*◊ no longer has the power to shock those who hear it.

Long established religions have been unable to keep pace with the changing times. The original aim of Buddhism was to explain how to gain liberation from the fourfold suffering of birth, aging, illness, and death. But Buddhism shifted its stance to the funeral rite after death and to memorial services. Having lost sight of its goal, it merely repeats its sermons of practical instruction. But in a world unrelated to those priests, an old lady washes *daikon* radishes in the midst of the falling sleet. From her lips fall the words, "*Namandabu*,"◊ almost as often as the remaining leaves fall from the branch tips.

The sleet's falling today.

Whenever I see it, I'm reminded of Kenji Miyazawa's poem:

The Morning We Parted Forever◊

This morning

Sis's going far, far away

The sleet's falling, making it strangely bright outside.

> *That rainy snowy stuff — get me some, will you, Kenja.*

Thin rouge tint, when'd it get that way?

—coming from that gloomy cloud.

The sleet's falling in big wet splots.

> *That rainy snowy stuff — get me some, will you, Kenja.*

Remember those two porcelain bowls, the chipped ones

With the blue *junsai* pattern on them —

I'd use them to get the rainy snowy stuff you wanted to eat.

I'd fly off like a crazy bullet from a gun,

Right into the middle of that dark sleet.

That rainy snowy stuff — get me some, will you, Kenja.

From the dark bismuth-colored clouds

The sleet sifts out in big wet splotches.

O Toshiko!

As you lay dying,

To brighten my life

You ask me

For this refreshing bowlful.

Thank you, brave little sister.

Let me live a life guided by your love.

That rainy snowy stuff — get me some, will you, Kenja.

In a lull in that awful fever and tortured breathing,

You asked me for this,

This last bowlful of snow.

O Milky Way and Sun,

Tumbling down from the sky of that atmospheric world!

The sleet's lonely as can be.

I stand precariously

On two blocks of granite,

Where the two elements of snow and water come together,

This branch of glistening pine is

Covered with snow drops of ice-cold water — this

I receive this — the last thing my gentle little sister will ever have.

Throughout the time we grew up together,

We used these bowls so often,

> the ones with the indigo blue mark,

On this day, though, you must say goodbye to that mark.

> *Kenja, I'm going it alone.*

It's so hard to believe that we must part this morning.

In the isolated hospital room,

Beyond the dark divider, inside a mosquito net,

Lay my brave and gentle little sister, pale, sick,

Burning with fever.

Everywhere I looked to collect the snow

It was pure white.

The beautiful snow

From that dreadful, distressing sky.

> *I'm going to be born again, Kenja*
> *and it won't be like this,*
> *suffering all the time.*

As I look at you with these two bowls of snow

I pray from my heart:

May this somehow become ice cream in Heaven

That you partake this holy meal and share it with all.

I give everything I have to realize this wish.

Whenever I read this poem, a chill runs through me. It's not only so sad that it's beautiful, but for someone who grew up with the sleet, it captures the coldness of the sleet as well its odorless odor.

When his beloved little sister Toshiko died, Miyazawa is said to have composed as elegies to her the poems "The Morning We Parted Forever," "Pine Needles," and "Voiceless Grief" in the space of a single night. From Miyazawa's perspective as an ardent Buddhist and poet, this poem drifts toward the theme of the boundlessness of death, and passing through the transparent sleet, he produces a beautiful work filled with the light of compassion.

It's neither snow nor rain, and if you hold it in your hand it turns to water — that's sleet. If we could freeze the motion of the sleet falling from the sky by taking pictures of it second after second with a still frame camera, we might see it as snow or as water or as ice. But within the frame of time, it undergoes constant and uninterrupted change.

This kind of change is expressed by the word impermanence.◊ That all things are impermanent expresses the truth that all things and events in the world undergo a continual process of change, never stopping even for a moment. This word finds a special place in the hearts of the Japanese people, who like to talk about the changes of the season, and the life and death process of human life. For them the transiency of things and their evanescent quality express something of the beautiful. Today, though, the tendency is to place value on life alone, and since we ground ourselves in the assumption that we should never change, this word, impermanence, might as well be a term from a dead language.

The new leaves of spring are beautiful; the autumn leaves in the fall are beautiful; the empty tree of winter is also beautiful. Reflected in the same eye is the assumption that youth is beautiful, old age is ugly, and mourning over death is unpleasant. Reflected in the eye attached to the pleasures of life, the sleet appears dark and grim. Reflected in Miyazawa's eye, though, is the sense that both the sleet and death are transparently beautiful.

Chapter 2

WHAT DYING MEANS

> *"I can't tell you just how fine*
> *I am—a pity, really.*
> *From your point of view*
> *I must appear a terrible sight.*
> *From what I can see though,*
> *It's as I said: There's nothing*
> *but beautiful blue sky*
> *And transparent wind."*

Somewhere along the way I picked up a reputation for being an expert at handling corpses. And so anytime something unusual turned up, I was the first one they'd call. I ended up going to all kinds of places.

Nowadays all I need to hear is the destination and I can pretty much tell what kind of corpse to expect. If it's the tracks or railroad crossing, you figure it's someone run over by a train. The harbor or shoreline, someone who's drowned. You make an educated guess, pick out the equipment you need, and head out for the site. In the case of routine traffic fatalities, these are pretty much covered by ambulances shuttling them off to the hospital. Most cases requiring on-the-spot coffining are the unusual ones requiring police postmortem.

I got a call from the police today, asking me to bring a coffin on the double. The site was a seaside locale—someone drowned, I thought—and so preparing accordingly, I headed out.

It was dusk. As I got closer, I could see the police cars with their swirling red lights in a cluster of pine trees on a sea cliff. In the middle of the trees was a white sedan with policemen standing around it. Intuition told me it was a suicide by carbon monoxide poisoning. Among corpses, the suicides by gassing are the most beautiful if found soon enough. But let them go undetected too long during the hot summer days and you end up with a corpse so gone you can't even touch it.

As I unloaded the coffin next to the car, a patrolman came up to me and pointed up. From a branch of the pine tree was a body hanging by its neck. In this kind of case, the police investigative team usually arrives first and does their business, leaving the corpse wrapped in a blanket. But I had gotten there before them. After a while, a police van pulled up with a ladder. Nobody wanted to touch this corpse. But someone had to do it. After a while I noticed it was always the same people who ended up doing the dirty work. The young cops all suited up with rubber gloves and facemasks just end up holding the flashlight and never lay a finger on the corpse.

The other day we had a suicide case, someone had jumped in front of an oncoming train. Walking along the tracks with me, plastic bag in hand, was veteran inspector S. The skull had split open, scattering brain matter like white cod roe between the ties. We broke off some branches from trees growing along the tracks and used them as tongs to pick up the pieces. By that time me and inspector S were the only ones left.

There's actually no reason why I should be doing any of this. My job is just to load the corpse into the coffin and deliver it to the legal forensics department at the university. I don't have to help out. But when I get to the site, for some reason I feel obliged to lend a hand.

One o'clock in the morning. I got a telephone call from the company people on swing shift. Someone just contacted them saying their coffin exploded. They want me to go over there to check it out. This was the house where I just did a coffining the evening before. As I pulled up in front of the house, I saw all the lights on inside and everyone standing outside.

When I asked what happened, they said excitedly, "The coffin blew up!" Why, that's impossible, I thought to myself, but when I walked into the room where the funeral altar had been set up, I saw the flowers and funeral fittings scattered all over the place. As I looked closer I saw that the coffin had been split open as if by an explosion, the hand of the deceased protruding from one of the cracks.

The stench of the corpse was terrible. It was so bad I was almost ready to heave. Then I noticed the masking tape wrapped around the coffin lid. The masking tape was the cause. During the wake the stench of death was so bad we decided to seal the coffin using masking tape to make it airtight. It caused the dry ice and the gasses that the corpse emitted to fill the coffin to the point of bursting. At two in the morning I had to redo the coffin.

It was the body of a father who had died trying to save his drowning child at the beach. The child was saved, but the father was listed as missing. A month later his body washed up on the rocks at Cape Oyashirazu. The drowned corpse was so rotten that his face was in no condition to be viewed. Their eldest daughter, probably a college student, had rushed home from Tokyo. Weeping and crying, "Papa!" she pleaded with me frantically to open the lid. Her mother understood it was better not to view the body, but she was so affected by her daughter's emotional outburst that she instructed me to let her daughter see. When I raised the coffin lid, the girl took one look and saying, "Wh-what . . .," slumped down unconscious. All this took place the night before last.

I placed the deceased in a new coffin, redid the altar setting, and took my leave, telling the family that the person in charge would be here as soon as it was light outside. When I got outside, the dawn was breaking. On the way home, even while driving the stench kept bothering me. I got home, showered, changed all my clothes down to the skin and went to bed. But I still couldn't get rid of it. I was trying to get some sleep, but that stench kept waking me up. Then I remembered. It was my nostrils. I went and washed and trimmed my nostrils as best I could, and that did the trick. The stench was gone.

Had another unusual encounter today. Got a call from the police asking me to bring a coffin. When I got there, there was a throng of police officers and local people in front of an old, one-story house. The windows and entrance way were thrown wide open. When I asked what happened, they told me there was a terrible corpse inside. It seems an old pensioner living alone had died, and no one had noticed it for several months.

I peeked in through an open window. There in the middle of what appeared to be a storage room was a futon. It seemed the corpse was a part of it. I could see the mound of the covers under which the corpse lay, but, squinting my eyes, I seemed to detect motion from on top of the covers. Not only that, it seemed there were tiny white beads scattered throughout the entire room. One good hard look and I finally realized they were maggots. The maggots were coming out of the futon, spreading out into the room, and even crawling into the hallway.

A chill ran down my spine. When I asked the young policeman next to me, "What are you going to do?" he gave me a look of despair. He said, "I don't know how to do it; just get the body into the coffin." Using the radio transmitter in the patrol car, I called the company and asked them to bring me a broom, a dustpan, and a vinyl body bag.

At any rate we couldn't get near the body until we did something about those maggots. First, I started sweeping the maggots from the entranceway to the hallway, picking them up with the dustpan. It took an hour before we could lay the coffin down next to the futon. The coffin in place, I threw open the covers and was momentarily stunned. The policeman behind me averted his eyes and started backing away. The guy who brought me the broom fled outside. There were countless maggots wriggling like waves in the rib cage.

With a policeman holding the corners of the futon, we poured the contents into the coffin. Even after the coffin was on its way to university forensics, I was still cleaning up the maggots. As I was just dealing with maggots, one of the neighbor ladies began to help out with a broom and dustpan. Saying she lived nearby but didn't notice anything out of the ordinary, she gave a long account of how the old man was hospitalized before, so she thought he was hospitalized again. Or else how he might have gone to see his adopted son in Tokyo, or so she thought, she said, as she was sweeping up the maggots.

There was no need for me to stick around to clean up the maggots, but it was possible the site would be used for the funeral, so I started sweeping them up just in case. As I was sweeping them together, I got a better look at the maggots as individual existences. I noticed some were trying to crawl up the pillars to get away. A maggot is just another life form. And just when I was thinking that, I was sure I saw one of them glow with light.

━━

When you die, you want to die a beautiful death. But what makes for a beautiful death is not always clear. To die without suffering, to die without causing trouble to others, to die leaving behind a beautiful corpse, to die looking good — it's not clear what is meant by a beautiful death. Does a beautiful death refer to the way you die or the condition of your corpse after death? This distinction is not clear. And when you start to stretch the image of death to the method of how to dispose of your corpse as befitting your image of death, everything grows completely out of hand.

⊷⊷⊷

At the research foundation of the medical university in our area, I struck up a conversation with an anatomy professor whom I met in the prep room named Dr. M. He was involved in a program to get people to donate their bodies to science. At the time I met him, he was spending all his time and energy systematically registering body donors so that the medical school would meet the criteria of having a steady supply of donors.

The day a person I introduced to him registered himself as a body donor, he said to me, "Thank you for your help! Say, what do you think of all this? Right now fifty percent of the registered donors in the White Lily Society are Christians. Christians don't even add up to one percent of the people in this area. And it was Shinran who said, 'When my eyes close for the last time, place my body in the Kamo River, so the fish can feed on it'! The followers of Shinran's Jodo Shinshu◊ make up eighty percent of the people in the

Hokuriku area." Citing figures in a scholarly way, Dr. M spoke passionately of these matters.

At a later date, when the registered donor died, we had a chance to meet again at the preparations for the funeral. Our late father was a registered body donor, said one of the surviving family members, and so how do we go about it? It was late at night, but when I put in a call to Dr. M at his place, he came quickly by taxi. He explained that the funeral ceremony would be performed as usual. The only change was that, when the casket was sent off, instead of going to the crematorium, it would be taken by hearse to the university. Three years later the ashes of the deceased would be returned to the family. Every year the university holds a joint memorial service◊ for all donors. As he finished his talk, Dr. M humbly made his request again placing both hands on the tatami mat and saying, "On behalf of medical science, on behalf of our young medical students, I wish to ask you for your cooperation."

But then a woman whose face had become flushed, stood up and said, "I'm against it, completely and totally against it. I just can't stand to think of Daddy's body ending up cut into itty-bitty little pieces . . ." After saying that, she flung herself onto the body of the deceased and started to cry. After awhile all the family and relatives began to talk among themselves in hushed tones, and in the end they decided the original plan to donate the body was out. Even now, I remember how crushed Dr. M looked, his shoulders literally drooping as he left the room.

It's hard to change people's image of death. This is because it's tied up with what happens to them after death.

Recently, I read in the newspaper that in a village in China, the administrators announced that burials would no longer be permitted after a certain date, and that all bodies had to be cremated. But many of the elderly believed that cremation meant they would be unable to go to Heaven, and so they started to commit suicide one after another.

In one province it was announced that the new proposal would go into effect in fifteen days, and that in accordance with government regulation the burials would be replaced by cremation as of the first of next month. Among the elderly who heard this news, some crawled into their coffins after taking an overdose of sleeping pills, some threw themselves into the river, some had their final meal laced with poison, others went on a fast and died. It was reported that during the fifteen-day period 67 people committed suicide.

It's a bit frightening to think about how attached people become to themselves, that they should fret over how their corpses are to be disposed of after they die, that they want their will to be carried out, even as they walk to the brink of death. As to how the corpse is disposed of, humankind has devised various methods of earth, fire, sea, wind, and sky burial, depending on prevailing customs, culture, and religion.

The kanji for burial 葬 *so* is made up of the kanji for

death 死 *shi* sandwiched between two characters for "grass" at the top ⺿ and bottom. 艹 We can extrapolate from this that at the time the kanji for burial 葬 was conceived, the practice of burying the dead was to abandon the corpse among the meadow grasses.

At any rate, once a particular concept is firmly etched in people's minds, there's nothing that will change it, come hell or high water. The same goes for the image of dying a beautiful death. Although we speak of dying a beautiful death, what it involves varies from person to person, depending on world-view, religious outlook, and aesthetic sensibilities. This is also affected by how a person absorbs the customs and society in which he lives.

And so there's no universal criterion for dying a beautiful death. But in a certain age and in a certain society, there are definite tendencies that suggest themselves as the elements of a beautiful death. For instance, during World War II, death was praised in the words of the *Hagakure*,◊ "The Way of the Warrior is to always be prepared to die." Rather than live a long life, it was thought far more beautiful to choose a splendid death. Taking one's own life by *hara-kiri* or dying heroically as a *kamikaze* pilot was regarded as the more sublime form of death.

But after Japan lost the war, the old value system came crumbling down. Everything was turned topsy-turvy, and life was now seen as good and death in all its forms as despicable.

In a world that now placed absolute value on Life, one of the most shocking events for people at that time was the suicide by *harakiri*◊ by the writer Yukio Mishima, at the Eastern Division Headquarters of the Japanese Self-Defense Forces in Tokyo on November 25, 1970.

Mishima explains in his own work, *For Love of Country:*◊

> One of the ideas I have difficulty curing myself of is that the aged are forever ugly, the young are forever beautiful. The wisdom of the aged is always lost in a dense fog; the actions of the young are always transparent. And so, the longer one lives, the worse one gets, that is, life is nothing but one long slide downhill at the end of which we become the exact opposite of what we were. *For Love of Country* portrays a first lieutenant and his wife in a terrible predicament at what they do not realize is the high point of their life. While they go on to die the ideal death, I attempt to place their greatest physical pleasure and their greatest physical suffering under the same principle. Thus, the circumstances for their ideal death could well have been set against the February 26th Incident◊ of 1936.

In *Kyoko's House,*◊ he says,

> If we consider the proposition that the human body is indeed a work of art, then is there no way to stop

the corrosion that takes place in the course of time? If this proposition holds true, the only way to escape this fate would be to commit suicide when one is at peak condition.

This story relates the double suicide of two young lovers. For Yukio Mishima, the only way to achieve a beautiful death was to commit suicide.

In Shichiro Fukazawa's, *The Ballad of Narayama,*◊ the action performed is the same, the protagonist choosing death over living a long life, but the consequences are entirely different. In *The Ballad of Narayama*, aged Grandma Orin thinks that rather than dragging out her life for as long as possible, it's better for her to die: "I've been in the village so long now it puts a strain on everyone. I've come to the age I should ascend the mountain where the old are left to die." And so she asks her son to take her there as soon as possible. Here, as Grandma Orin approaches the summit of Narayama where she is to await her death, she thinks it a beautiful way to die.

When this work won Chuokoron's Best New Author Award, Yukio Mishima was one of the members on the selection board. His appraisal of the book was as follows:

> When I read this book the impression I got was what a gloomy, musty feeling it has to it! I felt like I was being dragged to the bottom of a dark swamp. It's beautiful but — and this is my own personal sentiment — it gives me the willies, and I get this sunken feeling like when I

read *Sermon Ballad*◊ or *Winter River*◊ or Shinran's *Wasan.*◊

It has the same numbing effect on me.

The world described by Shichiro Fukuzawa in this work was one that Yukio Mishima was fundamentally opposed to. Orin's death was one of self-sacrifice out of love for the world of the living; Mishima's death was done out of love of self, such love cutting itself off from the perpetuation of life. From another perspective, Orin's death is the death of a person living in the fabric of a collective society; Mishima's death is of a special kind, the death of an alienated contemporary intellectual. In fact, no form of death places a greater burden on society than suicide. For the act of suicide is the way a person seeks to resolve his alienation from a cooperative society.

In either case, the way of death is better described as full of pathos rather than beauty. One cannot bear to look at the form of the old woman vanishing in the snow falling on the mountaintop. But neither can one bear to look at Mishima's severed head as it rolls about the floor of army headquarters where it has been given the *coup de grace*.

Aside from special forms of death such as suicide or accidental death, the generally held concept of dying a beautiful death is to one day go all of sudden without pain, without growing senile, without being bedridden for a long time.

The number of plump corpses has been on the rise recently. These plumped-up, celadon-colored bodies take on the appearance of water-filled plastic bags. When I first started out washing and coffining corpses early in 1965, the majority of cases were home deaths. I'd go to a farming home in the foothills to find a corpse with a withered frame like a dead tree. Even the complexion was dark, resembling the dried branch of a persimmon tree.

The deceased would be found recumbent in a dark room in the back where the Buddhist altar◊ was kept, the body forming a large letter L. This made for difficulties placing them in the coffin. Since their backs were bent like a shrimp, it was hard to get them to lie face up for viewing, and impossible for their faces to be seen through the coffin window. When their heads were in place their knees would stick up, and when their knees were in place their whole head would stick up, making it impossible to close the coffin lid. This testified to the kind of lives they led, bent over the fields from the time they were little until they died some decades later. There were once many such old farmers with crooked backs, and one could see the wisdom of using coffins where they can sit up. These round barrels like bathing tubs were the most suitable for the purpose.

The best word to describe the corpses of these old farm folks is "dried-up remains," for they looked like dried-up shells, the chrysalis from which the cicada had fled. Along with the economic advances of our country, though, we no longer see these corpses that look like dead trees.

Outside of traffic fatalities and suicides, almost all deaths today are hospital deaths. In olden days, when people could not take food orally, they invariably grew thin like dead trees. But now, with intravenous transfusions, making it possible for them to receive nutrition, they no longer fall into the extremely emaciated state we once saw. The corpses that leave the hospital are all plumped up, both arms blackened painfully by needle marks made at transfusion, some with catheters and tubes still dangling from throat or lower abdomen.

No matter how you look at it, it's altogether unnatural, as if a living tree has been split open. There's nothing natural about the way they die, as the image of dried leaves falling in late autumn would impart. This tells us that our medical facilities leave us no room to think of death.

The dying patient is surrounded by a medical staff who, with its life support systems, has only one thought in mind: to extend life as long as possible. Next is the family and relatives who think there's nothing more important than life. For the patients confronting death, they wait alone inside that cold equipment on a stage prepared to struggle against death. But even if they wanted to prepare themselves for death, there's no one to give them advice, and in that state they die.

Even if they wanted to talk it over with someone, there only returns the litany of "*Gambatte!*"◊ (Hang in there!) From morning to night, people recite to them the litany of "*Gambatte!*" as if the patient were an energetic young member of the company staff. Family and relatives come and say

"*Gambatte!*" Visitors come and say "*Gambatte!*" And in between nurses sometimes check in on you to say "*Gambatte!*"

I went to a symposium on terminal cancer patients, and about the only thing I remember was a statement made by Professor H from one of the national cancer centers. While attending an end stage patient, he noticed that every time someone said "*Gambatte!*" she would wince, and so once, after he had given her an injection to kill the pain, he told her, "I'll be following you on your journey," and that was the first time he saw her smile. After that he said that her outlook changed.

Doctors like these are few and far between, and so if you ever find yourself in intensive care, the upside is no visitors are allowed so you'll never hear anyone say "*Gambatte!*" The downside is you'll be surrounded by countless plastic tubes and cords connected to all sorts of instruments and monitors. When you accept the fact that your time has come and you start to drift toward the world of Light, the monitoring instruments at the nurse center will detect the change and set off an alarm. This will be followed by the hurried footsteps of nurses and doctors coming in your direction to shoot you up with injections and slap your face silly.

At any rate, it's as if someone were to come along and, without asking, suddenly change the channel of the television program you were watching. With the idea that life comes first, they place utmost importance on "saving life." Intruding upon a dimension rightfully ours, modern medicine robs us of the dignity of what people in the past regarded as most precious: that final moment of death.

In these circumstances there is no way we can die a beautiful death.

———

This morning, when I awoke, the snow was falling. It must have been snowing through the night. More than eight inches of snow had piled up in just one night. To anyone who ever grew up in snow country, this should come as no surprise. But whenever this snow-white world emerges suddenly before one's eyes, there's always a fresh sense of wonder.

Beyond the garden, camellias were blooming at the foot of the hedge. They'd been blooming there before, but I hadn't noticed them. It took this fresh background of fallen snow for their red petals to stand out. *Whoa!* I thought to myself, as I averted my eyes from the red petals, the piercing spectacle of the pure white landscape intruding.

I was just enjoying a quiet holiday for once when the telephone rang, disturbing my reverie. It was one of my relatives asking me to make a hospital call to that uncle of mine who was now hospitalized with cancer. It was years since we last met, the last time being when he broke off relations with me. I caught myself thinking something like, "Serves him right after what he did to me!" I still burned with indignity from that time. He called me a disgrace to the family; he made me crawl like a worm—that I could never forget.

Who do they think they are, anyway, telling me I should call on my uncle at the hospital! As I was clearing the snow from the car and shoveling the drifts of snow away from the house, I got another phone call. This time it was my mother. My mother had just gotten back from the hospital and was calling me right away.

"Can't you do it just this time . . . ."

"Hell, no. He's the one who told me not to show my face around here!"

"Well, you know your uncle looked after you when you were little. . . And you know today when I went to call on him he could barely tell who I was. He's so bad off, it'll probably be tonight or tomorrow . . . . "

As I listened to my mother's entreaties over the phone, I had a change of heart. If my uncle was in such critical condition that he could barely recognize my mother, it didn't matter whether he had lectured me or not. Besides, my auntie was always so good to me, and I bore her no grudge. I felt I'd better go to see him.

"All right, all right, I'm going, I'm going."

I put the receiver down and left for the hospital right away, not even telling my wife.

I was rather tense when I knocked at the door of the private room, from behind which my aunt peered out.

"Ah, you've come at a good time," she said, welcoming me in a big voice, explaining that he had been under but had just regained consciousness a little while ago.

Though I was a little concerned that I was making a bad entrance, my auntie took me by the hand and led me to the bedside. I could see that my uncle was definitely in a half-dazed condition. But he seemed to know who I was, and with both hands shaking he extended them upward to me. As I grasped his hands, I sat down on the chair my auntie had brought.

My uncle was looking in my direction and was trying to say something. His face was completely different from the face he made when lecturing me. It was a soft and gentle face. From the corner of his eyes a tear glistened. When I felt him grip my hands ever more slightly, I thought I heard him say "*Arigato*," thank you. Then later again, still grasping my hands, he repeated in a voice barely audible, "*Arigato*." That face of his was so soft and gentle, it virtually glowed.

The next morning my uncle died. The resentment in my heart was gone. The only thing I felt building up was a sense of shame. At the funeral, as I offered incense, I said, "Uncle, I am so sorry. Please forgive me." The tears were rolling down my cheeks in a steady stream.

It was a few days after my uncle's funeral. A package arrived in the mail; I hardly ever receive packages. The person who sent it was someone once close to me. When I opened the package a small book fell out. It was called *Thank You, Everyone*! It contains the last thoughts of a doctor named Kazukiyo Imura, who died at the young age of thirty-two.

I started flipping through the pages casually, but before I knew it I was reading it intently, sitting with back straight and legs tucked under me. Then, as I was reading it, it became impossible to go on, the tears were pouring out so fast I couldn't see the page.

> When I was told the cancer had metastasized to the lungs, I was prepared for it, but still the news sent a bit of a chill down my spine. After all, the cancer cells that had spread were in more than just one or two places. When I came out of the x-ray room, I promised myself that as long as I could walk, I would walk.
>
> On the evening of that day, as I was parking the car at the apartment, I saw a mysterious aura. Everything around me was extremely bright. The people going to the supermarket to shop appeared to be shining. The kids who were running around appeared to be shining. The dogs, the drooping heads of rice, the weeds, the telephone poles, even down to the tiny pebbles, all appeared to be shining. When I got back to the apartment, even my wife appeared to be shining, so much so that I wanted to put my hands together in reverence.

As I read this passage, I recalled my uncle's face. And I felt I had a glimpse from the inside why my uncle's face was so soft and pure. My uncle at that time must have seen my auntie, the hospital window, the flower vase, the nurse as if they were shining. That's why he had such a radiant and gentle countenance.

And then that word he whispered in a tiny voice, "*Arigato*," is repeated over and over again on the final pages of Dr. Imura's diary:

> Everyone, I thank you so very much. *Arigato*.
>
> The Hokuriku winter is serene. But having endured the
> long winter, the buds sprout after the snow melts,
> to proclaim the arrival of the tulip season.
>
> Thank you, everyone. *Arigato*.
>
> How wonderful you people are! Even as I was being
> battered by the waves that came one after another,
> you made sure that I was floating happily so that I
> would arrive at my final destination. How happy
> this has made me!
>
> Thank you, everyone!
>
> Thank you, everyone, thank you so very much. *Arigato*.

⎯⎯⎯

Day after day all I see are dead people. And so the dead appear to me as serene, even beautiful. By contrast, the despicableness of the living began to irk me—the living, who, out of their fear of death, peer into the faces of the dead with fear and trepidation in their eyes. As they watch me washing the deceased, I can sense their lines of sight mixed with feelings of alarm, fear, sadness, affection, and anger piercing me from behind.

Especially after my uncle's death and after I had read Dr. Imura's last thoughts, I became more conscious of the faces of the dead. When I think about it, up until today I've been in daily contact with the dead, and although I look at their faces, I feel I've never really looked into their faces. What people dislike, what they are afraid of, what they think unlucky they try to pass over without taking a good hard look. No doubt I too was acting instinctively by taking the attitude I did when handling corpses. Now, though, I am engrossed with the faces of the dead.

Though the faces of the dead engross me, in the course of being in contact with the dead on a daily basis, I began to notice that the faces of the dead were invariably gentle ones. During their lives I don't know what right or wrong they might have done, but it seems to have no bearing on them now. It doesn't matter whether their beliefs were thick or thin, whether they belonged to this denomination or that, whether they were interested in religion or not. Nothing they have done goes to making the dead wear such gentle faces.

In this part of the country, eighty percent of the funerals are Jodo Shinshu. This might lead one to think there are many devout Jodo Shinshu followers here, but that's not necessarily the case. What invariably happens is that it's not until someone in the family dies that people become aware they are members of the denomination. They attend the funerals of others, and while holding the Buddhist *ojuzu*, they put their palms together in a gesture of reverence. But they are believers who do not believe in Amida Buddha◊ and have never chanted the Name of the Buddha.◊

Be that as it may, the faces of the dead all have the same gentle expression. At the time they die almost all of them have their eyes half-closed, exactly like well-executed statues of the Buddha.◊

There's a famous saying from the Jodo Shinshu treatise *Tannisho*◊ (Grievous Differences), "even a good person attains birth in the Pure Land.◊ So it goes without saying that an evil person will." Since I had no knowledge of Shinran's◊ thought in my student days, these words had fresh appeal to me.

But for someone like me who sees the faces of the dead on a daily basis, I would contend that it's more accurate to say there's no good person or evil person among those who die. There are many commentaries on *Tannisho*. Many of them say the good person relies on self-power in an effort to achieve birth in the Pure Land, while the evil person does not operate in that way. Various explanations are brought forth, but the peaceful composure of the faces of the dead are completely oblivious to these weary arguments.

The other day I did the coffining of a syndicate boss whose face in repose was truly peaceful. Someone told me that when he was young he spent a long time in prison for homicide.

It could well be that a person will take up arms for the sake of his country and yet return from war without killing a soul, while another soldier will loathe fighting yet will end up killing numerous people. It could well be that a person who seeks to help others will draw misfortune upon them, while another person who is cold to others will do much to save people.

Seen from the eyes of the Tathagatas and Bodhisattvas, there's no distinction of good or bad among people. There are only people caught in the wretched state of affairs growing out of their self-centered existences in a world where the strong prey on the weak. According to Shinran, if given the opportunity, even if we know what we're to engage in is ethically unconscionable, we will still do it, as Yuien explains in *Tannisho*. In his grasp of the matter, Shinran makes this statement neither from the standpoint of good nor from the standpoint of evil.

People who make their own standpoint the criterion for their thinking are used to making pronouncements on that basis. When a person makes a statement on good and evil, for instance, there's clearly a difference if that person thinks himself a good man or if he thinks himself evil, and this has important consequences for how we perceive that statement. Especially when making a statement on life and death, it becomes a one-sided statement based on the stance of life, since it's impossible for us to take the stance of death.

However, Shakyamuni◊ and Shinran express their ideas from a point transcending life and death. When we ask what kind of place this third position transcending good and evil and life and death can be, it would have to be a place where both good and evil and both life and death can be seen at the same time.

At some point or another these thoughts entered my mind, as I looked into the faces of the dead.

"After looking at the earth for one year, I gradually became aware of it as a fragile and dear thing." These are the words of Russian cosmonaut Vladimir Titov. We live on the earth, yet we never sense it as fragile and dear. If we were able to shift our perspective to see it from outer space, however, we would be able to sense the earth and be aware of it as such.

If we never shift our perspective from the standpoint of life, no matter how much we want to think on death, it will only be an extension of our thinking on life. Further, when a person talks about the world of death, it never goes beyond theories and propositions. Setting out on that journey to the under-world, we don a white pilgrim's robe, carry a staff, and have around our neck a small coin to pay for the ferry across the River Styx—these ideas are born out of an extension of our thinking on life.

In theoretical physics, if a new theory cannot be proven by experimentation it ends up being erased from history. But when it comes to the various notions of the afterlife, there's no way to demonstrate them, short of a miracle, hence these propositions float around, and over thousands of years they get skillfully woven into the legends and stories that exist in great profusion.

Whatever the period, people have persistently formulated their thoughts on death from the standpoint of life. As they view death from the perspective of life, they deal with death only superficially. The result is that the thoughts they formulate on death have no lasting value. This is especially true of many learned people who, in their emotional attachment to life, will assert that they firmly believe in the human ability to understand things, yet whose grasp of things in reality leaves much to be desired.

In the postwar period, contemporary poets struggled in vain to liberate themselves from the nihilism of the age. It may well have been they too were overly attached to life, such that it made them incapable of approaching death on its own terms. In this age when we are flooded with information, the vast majority of artists take man to be the measure of all things, their works from start to finish being, as it were, life-sized. As a result, they avert their eyes from looking at death directly and try to escape it. They attempt to see the world from the perspective of life alone.

On this point, Kenji Miyazawa opens up before our very eyes a world beyond that of man as the measure of all things. A scientist, a Buddhist, and a poet, Miyazawa says, "This phenomenon that I call 'myself' is but one instance of that blue luminescence that I had conjectured to be a flowing current of organic electrical light," and "A sense of the fourth dimension flows through and informs these static objects." He is a poet who speaks of the fourth dimension as one who's been there and back.

What is especially beautiful about Kenji Miyazawa's works is that, just when we think his line of vision is pursuing the world of the microscopic, he shifts to the solar system, the galaxy, the universe, and in the next instant he shifts focus to the elementary particle. That eye shifting freely from microcosm to macrocosm functions very much like a zoom lens.

In this capacity, his line of vision is like the eye of *Kannon*, the Bodhisattva of compassion whose eye is able to freely perceive the world that appears in *The Heart Sutra.*◊ It's by shifting one's perspective that a feeling of rapport with others is born. A feeling of rapport means to be able to stand in the other person's place. In Miyazawa's poem, *The Morning We Parted Forever*, as his sister Toshiko is dying, he attempts to become one with her in spirit and see things as she sees them. In his well-known poem *Don't Give In to the Rain,*◊ we also find a poem expressive of this sense of rapport with others. In his children's story, *Yodaka's Star*, Yodaka becomes a star when he realizes that the winged insects are also life forms and thus grows in rapport with them.

Out of this sense of rapport with living things that made him want to live and let live, Miyazawa refused to eat meat and pursued a life of vegetarianism. This was largely the cause of the illness that befell him, leading to his death at the young age of thirty-seven. Among the works he produced while in his sickbed are a number of mysterious poems such as the following:

It's no use,

There's no stopping it.

It keeps bubbling up in thick blobs.

Couldn't get to sleep last night,

I was bleeding so much.

Just beyond is a transparent blue.

Seems I'm going to die in a short while,

But what wind is that?

Spring is already upon me.

It's as if the sky itself has come gushing up

   for it to be this blue.

From that sky a beautiful breeze is coming,

The young shoots of maple and tresses of flowers

Are being set in motion like autumn grass.

Even the tatami mat with its burn marks appears blue.

You look like you just came back from a medical convention,

Judging from that black frock coat of yours.

Seeing that you've gone out of your way to provide me with

   all kinds of treatments,

You can be sure that I will die without complaining much.

Aside from the fact I'm bleeding all over the place

The reason I'm so lighthearted and hardly suffering at all is

Perhaps because the spirit has left me halfway.

And, because of all the blood I've lost,

I can't tell you just how fine I am—a pity, really.

From your point of view I must appear a terrible sight.

From what I can see, though,

It's as I said: There's nothing but beautiful blue sky

And transparent wind.

This poem was written by Kenji Miyazawa when he was bedridden in the hospital with a high fever. Refusing to eat meat, he had scurvy and was bleeding constantly from his gums. On top of that, he was stricken with tuberculosis and was coughing up blood. Since, at the time of his illness, he could neither speak nor write, the poem is titled *Telling It with My Eyes.◊*

This work is said to express Kenji Miyazawa's near-death experience. Miyazawa's perspective here is not that of the physical body lying on the hospital bed. He's already separated from the physical body and floating in space, from which perspective he can see the doctor and himself covered with blood. Further, he's not suffering and is where he can see the blue sky. When I first read this poem, I had been thinking what death was and what being born after death meant for some years, and I felt I got a solid hint from it.

There's a painting by Paul Gaugin with the long title, *"Where do we come from? What are we? Where are we going?"* It's his masterpiece from the time he was in Tahiti.

When I'm in the role of sending off the deceased at funerals, this question is always on my mind.

We can leave the question, "What are we?" to philosophers, but the question "Where are we going?" is one that looms before us at the sending off.

For instance, at a Jodo Shinshu funeral, everyone sends off the spirit of the deceased "to be received into the hands of the Buddha." This is followed by someone reading a eulogy that closes with the words, "O spirit, now you may rest in peace!" The family representative then says, "Father is now happily at rest beneath the sod." Thus, we think of the deceased as having been received into the hands of the Buddha, as floating in space, and as being buried beneath the sod.

Those who come to the funeral put their hands together in reverence before the body of the deceased, they put their hands together before a photograph of the deceased, they put their hands together before the altar and the hearse—they even put their hands together to the smoke trailing away from the crematory smokestacks. But very few put their hands together in *gassho*◊ before the image of the Buddha. The Buddhist priests are chanting a sutra, and since no one can understand what they're saying and no one knows where the deceased has gone, the people at the funeral just follow the lead of the other people as best they can.

In addition, in Buddhist thought there's the concept of the Intermediate State.◊ Those possessed of life traverse the six realms◊ of heavenly beings (*devas*), humans, fighting demons (*asuras*), animals, hungry ghosts (*pretas*), and hells where they are born and die, only to be born again in endless cycle.

From the end of one life to the beginning of the next there's an Intermediate State, said to last 49 days. The 49 days are divided into seven 7-day periods. At the end of each 7-day period it's possible for the soul to be reborn. But if, at the end of the 49-day period, the destiny of the soul has yet to be determined, that spirit is fated to wander about lost. And so even from this we cannot determine the answer to the question, "Where are we going?" Conscientious family and relatives will hold one-year, three-year, and fifty-year memorial services, a symbolic turning over of merit to the spirit of the deceased, but in the end we can never know whether that person became a Buddha or not.

There are some things better left unknown. If that destination on the six paths were known for certain, it's a foregone conclusion that our beloved members of family and relatives would end up in the realms of animals, hungry ghosts, and hells. For instance, if I knew that uncle of mine were to be reborn as a beast, I wouldn't be able to enjoy that French veal dish or that Chinese duck at the restaurant. So it's better not to know.

Ever since I got involved in the work of funeral services, one thing I found perplexing and even shocking was that, although the ceremonies were to all appearances done solemnly as if to hold deep meaning, in reality they were an incoherent mass of superstitions and folk beliefs. I couldn't help being impressed how skillfully these superstitions and folk beliefs were rendered into tangible form and worked in as features of the ceremonies.

People, thinking that death should be regarded as taboo, have filled the mountains and valleys with superstitions and folk beliefs, of all kinds. Death became a forbidden glade where none may enter, a secluded castle in a mystical realm. These superstitions date back thousands of years down to today's folk beliefs accumulating in great number. Thrown into this batch are elements of Japanese Shinto, Chinese Confucianism, and doctrines of various Japanese Buddhist schools, making for a strange and mysterious brew at the level of local culture.

What led to the conception of such funeral rights and customs is the vagueness surrounding the questions, "Where do we come from? What are we? Where are we going?" Almost all of the funeral rites and decorum are built on the assumption that when a person dies, the spirit of the deceased will wander about lost.

At the bedside of the deceased, only one stick of incense is burned at a time, and if you ask why not two sticks, they will tell you the spirit might become confused with two trails of smoke. If you ask why the funerary tablets are necessary, they will answer they provide a place where the spirit can dwell. The sixpence coin, the pilgrim's bag, the gloves and leggings, the cane and straw sandals, are all for the soul to use when it wakes to that trudging journey through the Intermediate State.

When the priest in charge of the ceremony arrives, it's for the purpose of guiding the spirit of the deceased across. Bellowing, "O spirit, be on your way to Buddhahood!" He urges the soul on, but whether that results in Buddhahood or not is something we can never know. It's because a person has not attained Buddhahood that the memorial services are done to provide the spirit with extra merit it can use on its journey.

One practice is to place a short sword on the breast of the deceased so that it can protect itself from spirits and obstacles on its journey. Another practice is to turn the folding screen upside-down next to the deceased. At any rate, there are all kinds of practices that one can make neither heads nor tails of.

The Buddhist funeral ceremonies practiced today are a far cry from the ideas espoused by Shakyamuni and Shinran. To put it in radical terms, they are no different content wise from the animism◊ and worship of the dead of primitive religions. The only place they differ are in their modern appearances.

In a time when science is unlocking the secrets of the universe and of life, the animism dwelling in the human heart has survived unchanged for thousands of years. This points to nothing other than the belief in the existence of a substantial human selfhood. This substantial selfhood is what lies behind superstitions and folk beliefs. It is the belief in the existence of a soul as an entity that can never be extinguished.

Shakyamuni, against the prevailing Brahmanic◊ belief that the soul exists and transmigrates, denied the existence of the soul or substantial selfhood, to proclaim a new Buddhist paradigm of nonself in interdependence.

Chapter 3

THE LIGHT AND LIFE

*"First, we lose our attachment
to Life; at the same time we lose
our fear of Death. Finally, we
feel peaceful and serene inside.
Forgiving of all things, we enter
a state where we hold all things
in gratitude."*

After you've been in this line of work for a while, it gets
to the point where you can gauge the degree of misery the
moment you step into the entrance way. Even before you step
into the house proper, you can sense the deep sorrow engulf-
ing a family who has suddenly lost someone dear to them.
The tension level of the house is so high you can almost taste
it. This was the kind of house I was calling on today.

A young couple were out on a drive with their two children
when they met with an accident. The two kids playing in the
backseat were not hurt, but the father who was driving was
injured seriously and the mother in the passenger seat was
thrown from the car and died instantly. She was the deceased.

In an inner room of the large farmhouse, lying on a *futon*
before the altar was the body of the woman with a bandage
around her head. A *haori*, half-coat, with the family crest was
placed upside down on the covers. At the pillow side of the

deceased, holding on to a small boy two or three years of age was an old woman sitting there visibly steeped in sorrow. Right next to her was a four- or five-year-old girl who kept standing up and sitting down.

Looking at the face of the deceased, a face that had sustained not a single scratch, it looked as if she might have bumped her head and was resting. "Mamma sleeping still?" the little girl said all of a sudden. This set off a round of sobbing everywhere in the room at which point the old woman fell to the ground, beating the *tatami* mat with her fists and wailing loudly. The coffining had to be put off for a while.

I finished the job surrounded by people sobbing and crying. I was about to go to the lavatory to wash my hands when a man who appeared to be the village head stopped me and led me to the garden out back. Filling a plastic bucket with cold water, he topped it off with hot water from a large tea kettle, and told me to dump the dirty water in the bamboo grove after I'd finished. "Local custom," he said, and then he disappeared.

Just as I finished pouring out the water in the bamboo grove, something shiny passed right in front of my eyes. When I looked closely, I saw it was a delicate dragonfly fluttering weakly amongst the bamboo. After a while it stopped to rest on the dark green trunk of this year's bamboo. Peering at it close-up, I could see the translucent blue body of the dragonfly was completely filled inside with eggs.

Just a short time ago as I was doing the coffining surrounded by people crying, no tears came, but when I saw the eggs shining in this dragonfly, tears filled my eyes. This tiny dragonfly dying after a few weeks has been bearing eggs in unbroken succession to perpetuate its life form from hundreds of millions of years past. As I thought of this, tears started to come out nonstop.

Outside the Train Window

Outside the train window,
The world is filled with light,
The world is filled with joy.
How vibrantly life goes on!
And so when I think,
I'm to say farewell to this world,
That sight I've seen a hundred times
Suddenly presents itself anew.
This world
Of people and nature
Is so filled with happiness,
And yet I must die.
And that's what makes this world truly happy.
That's what comforts me in my sadness.
My breast heaves with emotion,
I'm so choked up, tears fill my eyes. . . . .

This poem is from Jun Takami's collection *From the Brink of Death* which was published one year before the author's death from throat cancer in 1965. In the early postwar period, Jun Takami, stricken with tuberculosis faced death, and then ten years later he was stricken with cancer, again suffering the fate of having to look death in the eyes.

I've been looking at death close-up all day long for ten years, but it's always been someone else's, not my own. But when I thought of the glowing light of the maggot that I saw when sweeping up, or the light I saw in the dragonfly in the bamboo grove, or the light Dr. Imura saw filling the world in the parking lot, or the light Jun Takami saw outside the train window, I could not help but feel they were qualitatively one and the same Light. In each case it was the same, I was moved to tears, so much so I started crying and couldn't stop.

I wondered if, as you approach death and are staring death in the eyes, all things begin to shine on their own. As to what sort of light, well, I'd be hard put to say what it was in so many words. But I thought I could detect in the face of my uncle as he grasped my hand and said, *"Arigato,"* and in the faces of many of the deceased, the glimmering traces of that radiant light floating about.

It could be that, when we are fighting one on one with death, at the bitter end we come to a point where Life and Death resolve themselves, and in that moment we encounter that mysterious Light. It could be that when we accept death and allow it to enter our confines, in that instant a mysterious transformation takes place.

Somewhere along the line, I started reading religious books. Stressed out, I used to reach for the *Tannisho*, but then it got to the point any kind of book would do, as long as it was on religion. So, reading up a storm, the best explanation I could find of that mysterious Light was by Shinran:

> The Buddha is what we thus come to experience as
>
> that mysterious Light; the Tathagata Buddha◊ [issuing
>
> from Reality-as-Such] that we thus come to experience
>
> is that Light.

Thus asserted Shinran, to make the clearest statement I have ever come across. His main work, called *Kyogyoshinsho,*◊ contains the basic philosophy upon which the present Jodo Shinshu school is founded.

The first thing you notice when you open the book is that the chapter, Teaching (*Kyo*), is extremely short next to the other five chapters. That's because Shinran starts off by presenting the conclusion to the entire *Kyogyoshinsho* first. The opening lines of the other five chapters are also very much like the one-line verdict the judge hands down when he passes sentence, followed by the long and detailed reasons for that verdict. Here Shinran is unlike Honen◊ who wrote his *Ichimai kishomon,*◊ or "One Sheet Document" and some scholars think Shinran belabors the point. For those who think so, I suggest that they not get caught up in all the reasons he gives, for he always sets down his conclusion first.

"The one work where I find the Teaching most truly expressed is in *The Larger Sutra of Infinite Life*."◊ Shinran is here setting out in clear and concise terms his conviction that *The Larger Sutra of Infinite Life* is where the Buddha most sincerely explains the Teaching to us. Then follows numerous sutra passages and commentaries that point to the reasons behind this choice. This is the structure of *Kyogyoshinsho's* first chapter.

My first reading of *Kyogyoshinsho* was fraught with difficulties. There was a lot I couldn't understand, so I read numerous commentaries. But then I noticed the commentaries invariably balked when it came to explaining what the Chapter on the Teaching was all about. At first I thought I'd made a bad choice of books, and so I'd look for another author. After awhile I had collected almost all the books there were on *Kyogyoshinsho*.

Whoever the commentator was, I could never get a clear explanation. Some even went so far as to say that the evidence Shinran presents is inadmissible, or that the method he applies is curious, comments which made eminent scholars of religion and Buddhist studies only shake their heads. That is, when we examine the grounds on which Shinran makes the claim that *The Larger Sutra of Infinite Life* contains the ultimate Teaching which Shakyamuni set down—out of all the teachings made during his lifetime—the reason Shinran gives is so unexpected, so out of the blue, that it seems completely illogical.

The reason Shinran gives is, "because Shakyamuni's face was radiant." He says the proof lies in *The Larger Sutra of Infinite Life*'s portrayal of the Shakyamuni Buddha's face as being radiant with light.◊ In *The Larger Sutra of Infinite Life*, there's a scene where the disciple Ananda is praised by Shakyamuni for noticing there's something extraordinary about the Buddha today, his face being radiant with the joy that fills his being. Seeing the serene light emanating from the Buddha, Ananda says, "What may I ask is the cause of your radiant expression?" whereupon the Buddha praises him, saying, "How astute of you, Ananda, to notice!" It was this scene alone, where the Buddha emerges with "a face radiant with light"◊ and Ananda is praised for his astuteness in noticing it, that made Shinran so sure *The Larger Sutra of Infinite Life* was truly and sincerely the Teaching.

I cannot tell you how moved I was when I first came across Shinran's treatment of this scene. And I realized at that point that Shinran's philosophy is one that grew out of his life experiences.

Buddhism is a religion that grew out of Shakyamuni's life experiences. Unless we remind ourselves of this — that it was not an idealized concept or a systematic philosophy — we will have great difficulty understanding the Zen◊ story of the Buddha "extending the flower with a smile"◊ or the exchange that took place between Shakyamuni and Ananda when the

Buddha emerged with "a face radiant with light."

Before Shinran was a great philosopher, we must remember that he was a sincerely religious person and that this was the life he led. Without a clear sense of religious conviction there's no way Shinran could have known from this one scene in *The Larger Sutra of Infinite Life* that this was the Teaching the Buddha truly and sincerely wanted to convey to us.

What history has handed down to us as the collected sutras of Mahayana Buddhism◊ were compiled into their present form some three or four hundred years after the death of Shakyamuni. These works were transmitted to other lands and cultures, and were affected by the demands of the written and spoken languages they donned. Ordinarily, it wouldn't occur to us to think we could gain insight into the Teaching the Buddha really wanted to convey by looking at these scenes describing the Shakyamuni Buddha. Indeed, this is something the researcher interested in the doctrinal conventions of the Buddhist canon can hardly understand.

But Shinran's take on the problem is completely different. I would assert that Shinran had an encounter with the Light, and from that glimpse of the Light got the inspiration to write his *Kyogyoshinsho*. Meeting the Light is meeting the Tathagata Buddha by which we come to experience Reality-as-Such. A glimpse of the world of Light is a glimpse of the Pure Land. I would assert that Shinran must have more than once experienced the Light that Dr. Imura encountered, the Light that

Jun Takami alludes to, that Kenji Miyazawa saw as the translucent world of sky and wind as he stood on the brink of death. Unless we reach this understanding, our problem will remain forever unresolved.

This mysterious Light is of such a different dimension altogether it cannot be grasped by the intellect. It cannot be understood unless we experience it for ourselves. Leading figures of various religions concur that at a certain point in their lives they met the Light. "I am the Light of the world," says Christ, and so say all teachers who experienced the Light and take it as their starting point, as in the words, "In beginning there was the Light."

We can say Shinran was also an experiencer of the Light. As Shinran portrays it as Inconceivable Light,◊ this Light is something we do not ordinarily see. This Light we cannot see is what the gods and the Buddhas themselves allude to.

> Truly, truly, I say to you, unless one is born anew,
> he cannot see the Kingdom of God.
> —*THE GOSPEL ACCORDING TO JOHN*, 3:3

> Though Buddha stands before you,
> you see not the Buddha.
> —*TATHAGATA'S◊ LIFE CHAPTER, THE LOTUS SUTRA◊*

In his poem "Spring and Ashura,"◊ Kenji Miyazawa engaged in Bodhisattva practice says:

> Brandishing his poverty,

> he looks straight at me, that peasant:
>
> But has he really the eye to see me?

In Saint-Exupery's *The Little Prince*, the Little Prince says:

> Yes, it's true, this house, this star,
>
> even this grain of sand,
>
> Has a beauty not apparent to the eye.

What's there but cannot be perceived with the physical eye is what humankind has from ages past called God or Buddha. Shinran calls this Unhindered Light and Inconceivable Light. He also makes frequent use of the Name formula, "O World-honored one, with the mind that is single, I take refuge in the Tathagata of Unhindered Light, filling the ten quarters," coined by Vasubandhu of fourth-century Northwest India.

This Tathagata Buddha◊ of Light is also explained in *The Larger Sutra of Infinite Life* as possessing of twelve qualities: Infinite, Unbounded, Unimpeded, Unrivaled, Lord of Flame, Serene, Joyful, Wisdom, Uninterrupted, Inconceivable, Ineffable, Beyond Sun and Moon. These are called the Twelve Lights in Shin Buddhism. Boundless, endless Light flowing freely everywhere, Light second to none in brightness, calm, joyfully overflowing Light of wisdom, Light that cannot be explained even if we had all the time in the world at our disposal. Even put in these terms, it becomes ever harder to grasp, for it lends itself to no image we can conceive.

However, if we begin with the *Kyogyoshinsho* or *Tannisho* and squint our eyes to see the total picture Shinran describes in his masterwork, there emerges an image of the world of the Buddha that Shinran based his thoughts on. That is, what Shinran left to posterity fits together in a purposeful way to form an image. As you deliberate on those seemingly contradictory aspects, you suddenly notice they issue from a single perspective. That is, once you take the stance that, "In the beginning Shinran worked with an image," everything falls into place.

We hardly notice it, but our behavior is being moderated by an image we have of ourselves. Rather than speak of what we do as behavior, it might be more correct to say we behave according to the image presenting itself to us in our brain.

Here is a familiar example men might relate to. That bar you go to all the time you like because the hostess who works there has a pleasing image. In the case of women, it's not a matter of left hemisphere versus right hemisphere, but a holistic image they have which translates into how they behave. If the image matches, then it's a pleasing image, if it doesn't it's a bad one. Images are also a kind of expectation we have for our lives. We might get married thinking the person we've found fits our plans perfectly, only to find out later, after having lived together, that the images we have of our lives are too different to be compatible; such a relation often ends in divorce.

A person who's losing his shirt gambling at the race tracks

or casinos will swear to give it up for good, but then the image of himself winning comes floating up to his mind, and the next thing you know he's slipping out the door.

In sports recently, the image training method has been adopted where athletes train with that "winning moment" in mind.

Another example is the "think and grow rich" philosophy of Napoleon Hill that had a great impact on business people everywhere. It urges you simply to have an image of yourself as a successful person and to never give up striving for success.

People are not the only ones who behave according to their image of themselves. Separate a newborn duckling from its parents and place it for awhile next to a person or a dog, and it will grow up following that person or dog around. I heard a story that if you want a pine tree to grow straight, the best way to do this is to plant a cedar tree next to it. Perhaps the pine gets an image of itself from the straight growing cedar.

What's frightening is that someone will appear on the scene who will turn the tables by using this image to control people. A charismatic person in the political arena or in religious circles will draw a rosy image for people in order to cleverly manipulate the good-intentioned but weak-willed to satisfy his own desires.

At any rate, we may conclude that the images people have are closely involved with how they behave. Even if the apparent ends to which they direct themselves are the same, the images that inform what they're doing can be entirely different.

Yukio Mishima's image of death and Shichiro Fukuzawa's image of death are very different. If the image is different at the initial stage, even if the works they produce deal with the same theme, qualitatively speaking they will result in entirely different works.

The image is a matter of destination or conclusion. First we have a destination in mind and then we decide the means to get there. It's never the other way around, where we decide the means first and then the destination. Once you decide you want to go to Kyoto, you can buy a ticket. Buy a ticket at random, and you can hardly expect to end up in Kyoto. Some of the confusion that established religious institutions are experiencing today seems to be the problem that they have busy conferences on determining the means to get there, when their ultimate destination is not clear to them. They have only a dim image of where they want to go or what they want to achieve.

There's no fixed date as to when Shinran completed his *Kyogyoshinsho*. The usual explanation is that he did a rough draft while in Hitachi, or present day Tokyo, and completed it in Kyoto where he returned after he was past age sixty. In either case, if we note the fact he was into his fifties, we can say that this work was a product of his mature years, this being an age when fifty years was the average life-span. The images of a true Buddha land and Amida Buddha clearly informed his thoughts, and in this state of mind where they existed as veritable realities for him, he began to write. It is thus clear that the thoughts he set down were guided by a foregone conclusion.

———

The breeze was glittering. The fluffy cumulus clouds that were there a moment ago were nowhere to be seen, and an azure sky spread out transparently. A jet stream had appeared across the sky. As the jet itself was nowhere to be seen now, it occurred to me that the long white cloud it left was clear evidence that a jet had been there. And even if that transparent Light were nowhere to be seen, it occurred to me from that "face radiant with light" I saw on my uncle, and from the accounts left by Dr. Imura and Jun Takami, there was clear evidence that this mysterious Light existed.

It's just like Shinran said when he called this Inconceivable Light, for when you meet this Light, mysterious things happen. First, we lose our attachment to Life; at the same time we lose our fear of Death. Finally, we feel peaceful and serene inside. Forgiving of all things, we enter a state where we hold all things in gratitude. When we encounter the Light, we naturally come to be so.

A person in critical condition suddenly has a bright, gentle expression on his face, and is saying, "Thank you." And even when speaking is no longer possible, this feeling of gratitude so fills him that he says it with his eyes. This situation is often reported by those who are with a dying person in his last moments. They come back saying things like, "He didn't have long, so I went over to see him, but when I saw him, wow, his face was shining just like the Buddha's!"

When we let go of our attachment to Life and are no longer afraid of Death, our mental afflictions◊ extinguished, we pass beyond the struggle between Life and Death. To become calm and peaceful within means we have attained Nirvana. To be forgiving of all things means we have gone beyond good and evil. To be brimming with gratitude for all things means to let our life energy be redirected.

When you look at matters this way, to meet with this Light is to attain in an instant the ultimate goal Mahayana Buddhism directs us toward. Shinran says, "In the space of an instant that the One Total Experience takes hold, you swiftly and truly attain the unsurpassed path; that's why it's called slipping beyond effortlessly." *Slipping beyond effortlessly* describes the phenomenon the Light ushers in. Slipping beyond effortlessly means transcendence attained by sliding through.

I have said that the phenomenon of feeling gratitude to all things is to let our life energy be directed. This directing of our energy is a key point in Jodo Shinshu. That's why Shinran says at the beginning of his *Kyogyoshinsho:*

> Reverently contemplating the true essence of the Pure
> Land way, I see that Amida's directing of virtue to

> sentient beings has two aspects: the aspect for our
> going forth to the Pure Land and the aspect for return
> to this world.

Thus writes Shinran, setting down the greatest characteristic of Jodo Shinshu: the two kinds of directing. This notion of the two kinds of directing is the conclusion to Shinran's entire philosophy; it is the conclusion toward which it gravitates.

What is so significant here is that, before Shinran, the directing meant turning over the good merit one had accumulated to become a buddha.◊ Shinran, though, turned this paradigm around: it is from the Buddha's side that the directing is done with the living beings as recipients. With forward directing as our gratitude to the Buddha, and return directing as the compassion received from Buddha, these two phases operate simultaneously. This was how Shinran understood the Buddha as Light. This characteristic is why Jodo Shinshu is called the philosophy of gratitude.

The Vow of Other Power has no relation to the will or actions of people. It would be better to say, rather, the Vow of the Buddha (universal truth) is the Inconceivable phenomenon the Light ushers in. To illustrate, here's the poetry of a woman with terminal cancer.

LifeDeath

If you come to terms
With what's called Death,
How much stronger does
So-called Life buoy up!

What was once in conflict
Fuses together,
Leaving me in peace —
    how inconceivable! . . . .

My Dear Friends

When you are dying
You gain a way of being
    that stands squarely in absolute equality.
Whoever it may be
You feel you must forgive them.
How your heart goes out to them,
To people passing you on the street.
Something of a warm feeling
Wells up from inside.

These poems were composed by Ayako Suzuki,
the wife of a Jodo Shinshu priest who learned she
was stricken with breast cancer. These were written
around the time she accepted her impending

death, after fighting cancer for four years. Her
poem continues.

> There's nothing I regret as I take my leave.
>
> I've lived a full life.
>
> Keisuke . . . Daisuke . . . Shinsuke . . .
>
> Mami, too . . . You, too.
>
> When I say, Namuamidabutsu, my wish is
>
> For all of you to become the many Buddhas
>
>> of Amida Buddha's world
>>
>> who say in praise, Namuamidabutsu◊.

> To be sure I can raise you well.
>
> This is what I'll do.
>
> Shinya, I will become your Namuamidabutsu.
>
> Keisuke, I will become your Namuamidabutsu.
>
> Daisuke, I will become your Namuamidabutsu.
>
> Shinsuke, I will become your Namuamidabutsu.
>
> Shingo, I will become your Namuamidabutsu. . . .
>
> To our followers and our friends,
>
>> I will become your Namuamidabutsu.
>
> Whenever you think of me,
>
> Say, if you would, a Namuamidabutsu for me.
>
> Always and ever I'll be with you with each time you say Namu.

Thus, a mother's love becomes the Buddha's love. The two
passages just presented are words issued by a person who

entrusted her entire life to Amida. These, then, are at the same time the words of the Buddha. This transformation of the mother's love into the Buddha's love is what Shinran calls *eko*◊ (the directing of merit by Amida's vow). While Shinran's meaning is an outflowing of gratitude toward all living things great and small, this is naturally permeated by the Vow of Amida Buddha (the universal Truth contained in the phenomenon of Light).

In actual practice, even in funeral rites the notion of *eko* is an underlying theme in the Jodo Shinshu funeral rite, as distinguished from the rites of other sects that stress guiding the departed soul to attaining Buddhahood. Since there's no guiding the soul anywhere, this does not call for a guide, but among the Jodo Shinshu priests there are many who are under the delusion they are actually assisting the process of the departed's impending Buddhahood. For those who hold to Other Power, it's the Tathagata that works out our Buddhahood, without our lifting a finger. The one who does all the footwork is the Tathagata.

One big feature of Shinran's philosophy is that, by meeting the Buddha of Light when a person passes into death, in that instant he or she becomes a buddha. Since it's the Tathagata who sees that the "soul" of the deceased instantly becomes a buddha, there's no need for a guide, nor is there any need for the deceased to be rigged up with various paraphernalia such as funerary tablets, handguards and leggings, sixpence coins, or walking sticks. Crossing the River Styx and meeting Yama the Lord of the Underworld is irrelevant. There's no need to perform services to supplement the "soul" of the deceased with good merit. That's why there are no services of this sort conducted in Jodo Shinshu, although there are memorial services and the commemorative service for Shinran. What all this means is that Shinran threw out the Chinese notion of the Ten Kings◊ of the Underworld with its Intermediate State that Buddhism picked up along the way as it was being propagated. But he did not go so far as to reject the Intermediate State entirely. Here, how we treat the Intermediate State becomes important as we attempt to grasp Shinran's philosophy.

In Japan, almost all religions are based on the assumption that once a person dies, their soul wanders about lost. This is why we perform various funerary practices, rituals, and rites related to the "soul" such as using just a single stick of incense (producing a single trail of smoke the soul follows) and having funerary tablets (where they can "reside") and performing services to send good merit (in case they need it). But Shinran totally rejects the idea that the soul wanders about lost for so many days or so many months.

Shinran's understanding of the Intermediate State can be seen in Kenji Miyazawa's poem *Telling It with My Eyes*, where he relates his near-death experience. When I have an out-of-body experience it's as if I'm floating in space for the duration.

As I float in space I can see myself as "a terrible sight" and I can see "the beautiful blue sky." From that vantage, while seeing that "terrible sight"of yourself in this world, you have a direct view of the "sky" of the Pure Land straight ahead, and nowhere is death to be found.

Things like the corpse, the spirit, and the afterlife may pique the interest of people living in this terrible world, but for one departed, all that awaits is a sphere of refreshing breeze bearing them away to a transparent world. Since there's no death in this world, we say they've gone off to be born. For Shakyamuni and Shinran, there's no leeway that allows a dwelling place for spirits or an afterlife. There's no room left for Death. The only thing there is, is Nirvana.

Of course, the corpse would be left. But after one has made the passage to a new Life in that world of Light, what's left is like the empty shell of the cicada. Shakyamuni told his followers to let the laymen dispose of his corpse. Shinran also said, "After my eyes have closed for the last time, place my body in the Kamo river and let the fish feed on it." He regarded his corpse as little more than an empty shell. Let me put it this way: if a person can treat his own corpse like an empty shell, that person is an enlightened one.

The Buddhist teachings Shakyamuni explained were invariably tied to practice, and it was in practice he found meaning. Questions unrelated to practice, such as metaphysical ones, he refused to answer. Shinran was also one who faithfully kept up this tradition, sincerely pursuing the path of a seeker. Thus, Shinran's images of the Pure Land, of the person who is sure to attain Buddhahood,◊ and of the Bodhisattva never deviate from the range of demonstrable truths. The person who is sure to attain Buddhahood refers to the Bodhisattva who has achieved awakening. A Bodhisattva is a person who has been promised he or she shall become a buddha.

From the time of Shakyamuni's appearance in this world to the time of Shinran's appearance, the mainstream of Buddhist thought had regarded the religious stage of the Bodhisattva as one in which difficult ascetic practices were done, with the Buddha occupying the next highest rank immediately above that. But Shinran noticed that people intently followed the changes coming over them in their final moments. He noticed that when they welcomed death into themselves (that is, when a dying person was just about to say the Nembutsu◊), they would experience the Unimpeded Light. Shinran was sure that, through that experience of Light, they had won a place amongst those who were sure to attain Buddhahood, and that they would go on to attain Buddhahood.

Monastics at the Enryakuji complex on Mount Hiei labeled the followers of the Unimpeded Light Group◊ as heretics. It would seem obvious that one reason the Nembutsu congregation was persecuted was its claim that even without practice they would naturally be among those who were sure to attain Buddhahood, which the monastics found most difficult to accept.

It stands to reason, if one wants to get the status of one certain to attain Buddhahood, everyone knows the ticket is the Path of Self-Perfection◊ where one undergoes rigorous practices. Less convincing is to get there by just saying the Nembutsu. Somehow, it just doesn't have the same punch. To the practicing monastics, Shinran was selling the Bodhisattva model short, which they thought was totally unacceptable.

Shinran's belief in Amida was founded on the firm conviction that, whoever one may be, he will surely meet the Unhindered Light, the Inconceivable Light. And then there were the excesses Shinran saw firsthand, having lived on Mount Hiei for twenty years. The monastics' halfhearted performance of ascetic practices was no match for the rigors of life endured by ordinary people. He had had his fill of that sort of life.

However much one mortified the flesh, water doesn't boil at one degree below the boiling point. Unless practice forced the penitent across the threshold of death, there was no assurance they would meet the Light, their run-of-the-mill practices being of no avail. To make matters worse, even if one were to die in the course of self-mortification, in the overwhelming majority of cases all the other dying people in the world instantly become buddhas anyway. If so, what's the point of doing all these practices in the first place? The risks we have to take on the Path of Self-Perfection are so great so as to make it meaningless.

The truth is, it's one thing to go into ascetic practices the way Shakyamuni did, but the ordinary monastic goes through the routine only halfway. He might look enlightened, but he's not, though he instructs others in how to become a buddha. This was the case eight centuries ago in Shinran's time and it's the same today.

To avoid misunderstanding, we mustn't forget that in Shakyamuni's forty-five-year career, from the time he stopped short of death in his ascetic practices and, bathed in the light of reality, was awakened to the way things truly are at age thirty-five, until the time his mortal frame reached its end at age eighty, his was a remarkable life that went beyond our ordinary existence in life-and-death. It's a rare feat indeed for someone to live the life of an enlightened one for forty-five years.

There are a lot of things to think about when it comes to being a person who's sure to attain Buddhahood.◊ I don't mean we have to draw the line somewhere between high and low, nothing like that. Here, everyone's a Bodhisattva, but when someone's dying, he is on the verge of becoming a buddha, which might happen six hours from now as in my uncle's case, or after a year or more like Kenji Miyazawa and Jun Takami. But people usually die in a hospital after being bedridden for some time.

These days we cling to dear life as long as the breath of life remains in us, and make no space for death to enter. Once the

Bodhisattva state is beginning to take hold, though, that's no time for us to be worrying about life support. But "life comes first" is the only thing people recognize, from family and relatives surrounding you who fear death, to the attending medical team sworn by oath to extend life. With everyone cheering life on, there's no time for us to look at death or to make peace with ourselves. In almost all cases, the dying person moves on to Buddhahood without finding peace in themselves. But the peaceful faces of the deceased remain as proof of their attainment of Buddhahood.

If we think of Shakyamuni's forty-five years of being surrounded by the Light and living with a heart detached from the afflictions of body, yet managing to keep himself alive physically, the only thing we can say about someone like him is that he was a living miracle. And he may well be the only human miracle that's ever occurred in the thousands of years of human history, though it's beyond a question of a doubt he existed. Shinran was clearly aware of this window opening onto reality when he wrote:

> Deep in the state of the Great Serenity◊
> The Buddha's radiant face was wondrous to behold,
> As Ananda astutely observed,
> Winning him praise from the Buddha
> For inquiring as to the matter.

In this wasan, where Ananda is being praised for his astuteness, Shinran so closely identifies with Ananda that it's as if he too were being praised. Here, Shakyamuni Buddha and Amida Buddha have a buddha-to-buddha meeting of minds to form a unity. This unity is to enter deep into the state of the Great Serenity known as Nirvana. As the words that issue from that point on are naturally the words of Truth the Tathagata seeks to impart to us, Shinran says *The Larger Sutra of Infinite Life* is the Teaching the Buddha truly wishes to convey. Shinran's entire philosophy can be found distilled in this radiant face of the Shakyamuni turned Buddha.

⊶⊷

> As for the New Year being happy, *Medetasa mo*
>
> Let it be swathed in mystery! *Chu kurai nari*
>
> That's my wish for the New Year. *Oraga haru*

This is the verse Issa Kobayashi,◊ composed as he greeted the new year in the first month of 1819. To understand this poem, first we have to figure out what Issa meant by "swathed in mystery," or *chu kurai*, a phrase in Shinshu regional dialect which means "vague" (*ayafuya*) and "subject to change." But just knowing what it means in dialect is not enough. We have to read the passage Issa wrote just before this verse:

> As the chilly wind whistles down upon our junk of a
>
> house, let us do it up in the time-honored tradition of
>
> all the junkmen in the world, neither putting up fresh

pine branches on the gate nor knocking the soot off from last year, and just as the snow-covered mountain path curves and disappears out of sight, this year too, as spring approaches, I find I'm completely at your mercy, and so I leave my destiny in your hands.◊

In this passage Issa wrote down before the verse given above, the emphasis is on *anata makase*, "I leave my destiny in your hands." Here *anata makase* is used to mean I leave my destiny in the hands of Amida Buddha. What Issa is saying here, then, is, since I place my life in Amida's hands, I can pass on year-end cleaning or doing the gate up with pine branches; all I need do is welcome the New Year just as I am. And so, I don't know whether or not the New Year will be a happy one, but this is the way I'm celebrating its arrival.

As for me, since I'm no Arthur Rimbaud◊ who as a poet wrote verse that would be eternally remembered and then put all of his energy into becoming a merchant making a livelihood in the real world, I'd have no choice but to pass through life in this vague, *ayafuya* fashion.

If people were simply to die from being denied time to themselves, the poets would be the first to go.

These are the words of the French poet Paul Eluard, and in them too we find a grain of truth.

If God and Buddhas are the Light, and Jesus and Shakyamuni are their legitimate children, then the poet is the child of the Light, born out of wedlock, who will grow up estranged from life. He is the love child of the gods, separated from mother and father while still an infant, and fated to grow up in life with his true identity hidden from those around him. That is his place in this world. A poet's lot is a miserable one. Just as sleet is neither rain nor snow, so too is the poet neither enlightened nor ordinary.

Shinran also had a similar perception of himself as being neither a priest nor a layman. He was this vague, *ayafuya* existence that was neither one nor the other. Seeing himself this way he called himself Shinran the Foolish and Stubble-headed.◊

> Oh, truly you worry me, Shinran, you baldish fool!
> There you go drowning again in the widespread ocean
>   of love and lust,
> There you go again wandering off into the peaks and
>   valleys of fame and fortune!
> I told you you've gotten a place as a person sure to
>   attain Buddhahood, but does that cause joy to rise up
>   in your heart?
> —No!
> It's true your life has gotten closer to reaching a correct
>   understanding, but that's not something that thrills
>   you, is it?
> Oh, how embarrassed I am to see your face, how it
>   pains me to think of what's become of you!

Here Shinran confesses that his life is a half-baked affair going nowhere; truly his life is, by his own account, one big mess.

Shinran and Dogen,◊ as well as Ryokan, all had eminently important roles in their communities, and all of them were poets in addition. From long ago, I've thought it a mysterious thing to be born in this world a poet. I lost my father when I was still small and later my mother left the house, and so as a boy I would sit with my back to the plastered wall of the storehouse and gaze at the setting sun, passing the time this way thinking what a mysterious thing it was to be a poet.

In more recent times, it occurred to me that the birth of a poet in the world may somehow be tied to that mysterious Light at some early stage in that person's life. That is, if you look at the poets of the world, the kind of life they lead is what comes out in their poetic works, but theirs are not beautiful lives, and there are hardly any who have had happy lives. This allows us to see a common pattern in the way these poets lived.

These poets are not attached to things, and as this force of habit is not a part of their lives, they tend to be more thoughtful of people and act kindly toward them. Whatever they do in the struggle to survive, they come out on the losing side. Being pure of heart, they long for what is beautiful. Being fond of wine, women, and song, they make a mess of their lives when they go on a binge. And for all the time they spend gazing at death, they cling so powerfully to life that it isn't funny. And as skilled as they are with words, in real life they say things people misunderstand and end up going through life alienated. Why do they let themselves get stuck in this miserable rut?

As I was thinking how all this was a mystery, it occurred to me that this must be tied to that mysterious Light. As they come upon the Light, their attachment to life has grown tenuous, and at the same time their fear of death has lessened. They have a feeling of being peaceful and serene, they are ready to forgive all, they are thoughtful of the circumstances of others, they have a feeling of being grateful to all things. In Buddhism, those who find themselves in these circumstances are called Bodhisattvas.

The monastics who follow the Path of Self-Perfection strive to reach this bodhisattvic state as their final goal, but in the present world the harsh reality is that, in order to survive, it's hard to hold on to that Bodhisattva heart for long. The thoughtfulness of the Bodhisattva, for instance, is to stand in the shoes of the other, completely. If we stand in the shoes of the cow, never would we be eating steak. A person who loves all living things would hardly think of killing one of them. Anyone who has ever tilled a field knows that every time you lean into that hoe you might kill a bug or a worm. And though some insects and birds destroy crops, it's just an arbitrary call humans make when we brand those creatures as harmful.

A Bodhisattva's heart is what we find as we look through the eyes of Misuzu Kaneko,◊ a gifted writer of children's poems who died in the 1920s at the young age of 26:

Oh, Those Little Fishes

Oh, how sorry I feel for those little fishes in the sea!

For we tend the rice we grow,

And raise the cows in meadows,

And even feed the carp in the pond.

But as so for those little fishes in the sea,

There's not a thing we do for them.

Not a single bad thing they do to us, but

They end up like this, getting eaten by me.

Oh, how really, really sorry I feel for those little fishes!

To sustain our own lives, we have no choice but to take the lives of other living things to keep ourselves alive. In this sense, if a Bodhisattva were to be given the physical form of a human, he would find it impossible to maintain his life.

In order for the monastics who seek to walk the Bodhisattva path to sustain their lives while carrying out their vow not to hurt any living thing, requires the practice of *dana*, or giving, on the part of the laity. In Shakyamuni's case, as he sat under the bodhi tree, he reached a point where he had strained his life systems to the very limit. Then out of nowhere appeared a young maiden who gave him a sip of milk. This is the origin of *dana*, giving.

If Shinran looked into what a Bodhisattva was all about, the more he found out, the more he would have been convinced it was not something he could possibly do, and if ever he imagined he could, he was only deceiving himself. Indeed, to do the austerities required by the Path of Self-Perfection, to attain awakening, was simply out of the question. Even Shakyamuni could not engage in the austerities to the point of dying. It was enough to follow Honen's instructions and believe in the Inconceivable Light. If it was enough for one to put his all into the Inconceivable Light as an ordinary person, he would have chosen to live in the light of Reality as such a person.

We may speculate that if those poets were exposed even to the glimmerings of that mysterious Light, this is what pre-disposed them to sad and miserable lives. There's no way you can live in this world with a heart full of charity such as Kenji Miyazawa reveals in his poem *Don't Give In to the Rain*. He also shows a kind of gentleness, for this is a poet who started off with the wrong idea of getting married and raising a family, entered the world of commercial business, and only ended up exasperating everyone in the process. The best way for a poet not to exasperate people is to become a beggar, or he should be lucky to meet a woman with extraordinary talents.

And why should things turn out this way? The Vow of the Tathagata Buddha of Light is built on the major premise that those who are sure to attain Buddhahood will straightway attain Buddhahood. Once taken up by the Tathagata Buddha's Vow, there's no going back. Simply put, one who has seen the

Buddha's Light knows the Buddha will never let him go. Whatever may befall the poet, the poet's soul will never be erased. That's why the bodhisattvic poet Kenji Miyazawa would let his projects come crashing down halfway through. If he hadn't had his inheritance and the backing of his kind-hearted parents—not being cut out to be a beggar—he would have starved to death in the fields.

But the truth is, a lot of things happen to the dying person. A person might meet the Light, but it's not always the case that the Light will enfold you and take you up. Some people have seen the Light and returned. It's what we today call a near-death experience.

According to personal accounts of near-death experiences, one thing virtually all of them have in common is that after passing through a long black tunnel, in the next instant, they found themselves in a bright world filled with light. And in that bright light they could see their father or grandmother who died, or a figure of Amida. In European countries Mary or the Cross appears, and sometimes there are fields of flowers with butterflies fluttering about. These variations occur according to area and individual, but they only appear in the presence of the Light. Thus what all these reports have in common is the world of Light.

One other thing only those who have seen this world of Light say is that once they had this near-death experience, they no longer thought death was something to be afraid of.

This is something to take note of.

Now, it's not always the case that poets will have near-death experiences, and just as Bodhisattvas are those who have met the Light of Absolute Reality, poets may be those who have merely been exposed to the weak glimmering of its rays.

Things that happen that affect the foundations of life during childhood could give rise to phenomena similar to the phenomenon of Light. For a child to lose his parents profoundly alters the course of his life. In the animal kingdom, for a young one to be separated from its parents means death. To be separated from the source of mother's milk is to have its food supply cut off, and an orphaned newborn soon becomes prey for other animals. Eminent religious figures such as Genshin,◊ Honen, Myoe,◊ Dogen, Ippen,◊ and Shinran all experienced separation from their parents by age ten. Rennyo◊ also was separated from his mother at a young age. The Light that appeared to them on that tragic day in childhood remained with them and continued to exert a great influence on their lives.

People today face death due to cancer or AIDS; before these it was tuberculosis. During the first half of the 20th Century in Japan, many young people faced death due to outbreaks of tuberculosis when a state program of "military power for national prosperity" forced them beyond their limits.

But above all, what has brought many people face to face with death is war. With so many men marching to war, most of them go off thinking their lives will somehow be spared. But when those fatal bullets strike and they are unable to draw their next breath, there's no chance for them to experience the phenomenon of Light. More than on the battlefield, where shots are being exchanged, it's among the routed on the Burma front or in the Siberian concentration camps, or the Auschwitz death camp that people, seeing death as their own death, met death directly for the first time. That they met death directly for the first time, doesn't mean they were at the level where they could think about death and discuss it. The moment was approaching when they had to decide whether or not they would take death into their entire existence as mortal beings.

Thus, the way poets are born is different, but especially the tragic separation from parents during childhood can trigger their meeting the Light that has consequences for their entire lives thereafter. Instances where parents are divorced, or the family business goes bankrupt, or the family is broken up, even where one is a descendant of a once proud family line— these were often seen in poets of past ages.

In addition, there are those who in their youth were stricken with tuberculosis or cancer or AIDS and faced death directly. There are those who were the sole survivors among all the war buddies of a special unit whose mission fell apart. There are those who bet their entire lives on love and lost. There are those who were disillusioned by the ineffectiveness of their social reform movement. There are those whose businesses went bankrupt. The causes are many. When the bad luck keeps piling up and the burden grows, that's when the Light begins to intensify.

The point these situations share in common is that death is approaching someone who has every reason to look forward to life. As the struggle between Life and Death ensues, a Light is released when Life and Death fuse that bathes a person in its rays. Thus a poet is born.

When poets are born, they enamor themselves of the arts such as poetry, music, painting, or writing. Even as they seek out these leisurely activities, they meet with opposition from those around them who force them to go into some real line of work that they're not really suited for. Our poet-to-be, following the dictates of society, ends up with some sort of job to support his wife and children. But all this runs against the Vow of the Tathagata Buddha of Light, and the more the poet struggles the deeper he sinks, until having exasperated everyone around him, he drops out of society, a frustrated individual.

You'd be lucky if you were like Kenji Miyazawa who had doting parents who approved of whatever he did, Miyazawa being a poet inspired by the *The Lotus Sutra* to live the Bodhisattva way. But there are many poets in the world who find themselves unable to write poetry, who fail at everything they try to do, who exasperate everyone they meet. In fact you'll find hoards of such tenderhearted poet types.

But we must also realize there are many whose lives suffer the after-effects of having been only weakly exposed to the phenomenon of Light. This is what's wreaking havoc on their lives. Spun about dizzily from the word "go," they don't know what's what anymore, and in that condition their lives come to an end.

━━

In science today, through phenomenal developments in molecular biology and medical science, it has been shown that the brain secretes morphine-like substances called endorphins when the human body directly confronts death. This biochemical substance works as a painkiller to produce a soothing effect on the body. The body is thus thought to have its own system for naturally resolving the distress and pain that accompany the physical death. Some researchers have even suggested the peaceful expression on the faces of the deceased may be due to the effects of endorphins.

At first glance it would seem science today has gone beyond philosophy and religion. But it only seems that way because philosophy and religion are standing still. What science covers is only a minuscule portion of the entire track, and so it really hasn't outdistanced anything.

We can be certain science will continue to progress rapidly, and it could well be that studies will prove the effects of endorphins in such things as "the biochemical mechanism of *satori*" or how it's possible to sit in meditation in the middle of a fire by "keeping a cool head to cool the flames."

Now we know that, however much life repeats its pattern of generation and extinction, its genetically coded information of DNA remains intact. This allows us to speculate that the Buddhist notion of transmigration◊ may well be demonstrated by molecular biology one day.

Indeed, science may even hold the key to explaining what Amida Buddha is. Thus, the degree to which religion can be proven by science may decide whether religion will remain in history or not. Religion could well criticize science for clambering up to its sacred altar with muddy boots and throwing back the curtain surrounding its deepest mystery. But here, religion has to respond by ridding itself of its superstitions and coming up with something that will stand up to scientific scrutiny.

> A religion that is not scientific is blind.
>
> Science without religion is dangerous.

So said Albert Einstein.◊ Before we look at what "Science without religion is dangerous" means, people in religion should appreciate the words, "A religion that is not scientific is blind."It's clear that science has to recognize its own limitations and step down. But it's also a fact that science today has developed at such blinding speed as to leave us bewildered.

Leading scientists today are beginning to discuss the world as a single total reality (what Buddhists call *Tathata*,◊ or

"Reality-as-Such"). Erwin Schrödinger,◊ the father of quantum theory, says:

> The subject and the object are one. It does not mean that the dimension separating the two has crumbled with the recent findings in physics. Why this is so is because that dimension never existed in the first place.

Around the time science textbooks were coming out with quarks and leptons, elementary particles making up electrons and neutrons, I remember having misgivings about it. It sounded so much like Buddhist atomic theory: that the entire universe is composed of the five basic elements of earth, water, fire, wind, and space.◊

Molecular biologists assert that the creation of life has no need for a creator god or to be surrounded in mystery. They believe that one of these days it will be possible to create primitive life in the laboratory. Astrophysicists are drafting a systematic statement describing the events from when the universe began up to the time it took its completed form.

The Catholic Church is just as concerned that these scientists are unravelling the mysteries of the origin of the universe as it was when Galileo declared the earth moves around the sun. Scientists say the present universe was formed approximately fifteen billion years ago in an event called the Big Bang and has been expanding ever since. When no counter theory could be found to the expanding universe theory, Pope Pius XII◊ made this statement:

In fact, it would seem that present-day science, with one sweeping step back across millions of centuries, has succeeded in bearing witness to the primordial *Fiat lux* uttered at the moment when, along with matter, there burst forth from nothing a sea of light and radiation, while the particles of chemical elements split and formed into millions of galaxies. . . [Science has] followed the course and direction of cosmic developments and just as it was able to get a glimpse of the term towards which these developments were inexorably leading, so also has it located too their beginning in time some 10 to 15 billion years ago. Thus, with the conclusiveness which is characteristic of physical proofs, it has confirmed the contingency of the universe and also the well-founded deduction as to the epoch when the cosmos came from the Hands of the Creator. Hence Creation took place in time. Therefore there is a Creator. Therefore God exists.

Thus declared the Pope in a Papal Bull at the Vatican Academy in 1951.

But in 1970, when the expanding universe theory was beginning to show fracture lines, the Pope granted an audience with a physicist named Dr. Stephen Hawking,◊ at which time the Pope made this piercing remark:

"It's excellent to do research on the direction the
universe has gone since the Big Bang, but it will not do
to explore the Big Bang itself. The reason I say this is
that this is the instant of Creation, accordingly it is
God's work."

But science, as it develops, pays no heed to what religion
demands. Even though the Pope may have celebrated the
expanding universe theory saying, "Therefore God exists," that
view was soon on shaky grounds as scientists began to
theorize that particles of radiation called neutrinos which
filled the universe had a mass that could be measured.
Tentatively, if out of the hundreds of thousands of neutrinos
that made up the electron, just one of them had a measurable
mass, that meant the expanding of the universe would come to
a halt, and soon scientists were singing to the tune of an oscil-
lating universe theory, throwing the Vatican into a quandary.
For if the universe has no beginning and no end but just keeps
repeating its pattern of generation and extinction over and
over, then there's no place for a Lord Creator to appear.

For those of us who live in this so-called triple world◊
where, as the Buddhist metaphor goes, we have churned
about in transmigration from time immemorial, we look to
religion for something absolute and unchanging. If the object
of our worship is always going extinct and changing on us,
well, that won't do. That becomes the cause of our disbelief.
Faith demands the Absolute.

Whatever the religion, once institutionalized, its object of worship becomes off-limits to change after it has been promoted among the people, even though it no longer suits the times. It becomes taboo to violate its sanctity, as the Pope pointed out when he said it will not do to explore the Big Bang itself. Shinran had something absolutely brilliant to say on this point.

For Shakyamuni, the entire universe was built around the theory of *pratityasamutpada*,◊ that all things exist in a state of mutual interdependence. Just as Shakyamuni taught his own philosophy of nonsubstantial self and cast out absurd notions and belief in the substantial self taught by Brahmanic institutions of the day, so too did Shinran make the Buddha of Light the centerpiece of the Buddhist teachings taught by Shakyamuni. From among countless works in the Buddhist canon, Shinran selected *The Larger Sutra of Infinite Life* as what the Buddha truly sought to teach solely on the basis of its "face radiant with light" passage. He praised those eminent figures of past ages who recognized the significance of the Buddha of Light, composing hymns to Nagarjuna, Vasubandhu, T'an-luan, Tao-ch'o, Shan-tao, Genshin, and Honen. Without apology, he threw out the superstitious elements and absurd beliefs of his time. Even with regard to the set phrasing of sacred texts in the Buddhist canons, he reworked their standard readings to give these a new twist in meaning such that the truth he believed was there would come shining through.

Shinran writes in his *Jinen honisho:*◊

> What we call the unsurpassed Buddha exists only as
> beyond form. As a buddha issuing from Reality-as-Such
> has no tangible form, we call it *jinen honi.* But when a
> buddha has a tangible form, this buddha is not called
> unsurpassed Nirvana.
>
> As the unsurpassed Buddha is formless and has yet
> to make its presence known to us, the first thing we must
> learn to do is to listen to the name of Amida Buddha.
>
> Amida Buddha informs us of *jinen honi* as it per-
> tains to us. Once we've gotten the gist of it, there's no
> need to read into every little thing the workings of
> *jinen honi.*
>
> To always be discussing *jinen honi,* is to take this
> working of no set form and to reduce it to the level of
> fixed form.

Shinran orders us "not to read [*jinen honi*] into every little thing," thus utterly smashing the idols we place before us.
He even refers to Amida Buddha as just a device to catch
our attention.

The Light of the Amida Buddha is not like candlelight or
sunlight; it's not a light we can detect with our eyes. Nor is it
like the first rays of the rising sun at New Year's that people

pray to from atop Mount Fuji or the Tateyamas. Nor is it like the last rays of the setting sun that fervent Nembutsu practicers who believed in a western Pure Land followed into the waters of Osaka Bay long ago. Shinran called it the Light transcending sun and moon, thus the Light is neither sunlight nor moonlight. A light beyond sun and moon would be the Light of eternity.

Scientists estimate the sun will exhaust all its hydrogen fuel in less than six billion years. That means even the sun is not forever. Of course, by the time it burns out, all life forms on earth will become completely extinct. In one work in the Buddhist canon, it says that 5,670,000,000 years after the death of Shakyamuni, the Bodhisattva Maitreya◊ will appear on earth. Since this is when all life forms will be extinguished, it could be that the Bodhisattva will be there to rescue them.

This Inconceivable Light is immeasurable, reaching everywhere without limit. It penetrates all things and has neither shape nor form. It exists in eternity. If we think of it as a light that comes to us from eternity, then it's constantly near us, constantly shining upon us.

Just as I was wondering whether or not such a light exists, one day, on February 23, 1987 to be exact, just upstream of the Jinzu River that flows next to our house, a tremendous event occurred at Kamiokande, the Tokyo University Space Radiation Facility located one thousand meters underground in the Mozumi mine shaft, that caught the attention of astronomers and physicists everywhere. The big news was that a mysterious elemental particle was observed that was neither light nor photon. It had no form or shape, it could pass right through anything. It had come whizzing by from 160,000 light years away, and went right through one side of the earth and out the other into outer space. This mysterious particle was called a neutrino, the existence of which was theoretically proven but not seen.

What made me interested in this mysterious neutrino was one of the characteristics of this elemental particle discussed in the newspaper write up: that it was born the moment a star in the universe dies. In the final, dying moments of a star, 99% of the massive energy released as the gravitational equilibrium breaks down is whisked away as neutrinos, the remaining one percent becoming shock waves that disintegrate the star, and so the star dies. And then, becoming a supernova, it once again begins to sparkle. By this time the neutrinos are whizzing their way through space at near light speed.

For instance, the neutrinos that burst from SN 1987A, in the Large Magellanic Cloud, continued flying through space at near light speed, and on February 23, 1987, they passed through the earth from the southern hemisphere and exited from the north. What is remarkable is that, at a density of sixteen billion neutrinos per square centimeter or upward of ten trillion per person, they went speeding through our bodies in that instant. Unimpeded, incomprehensible, unlimited, without shape or form, just like that.

Especially noteworthy is the fact that, in the Big Bang or the explosion of a supernova, the generation of neutrinos takes place the instant the life and death of a universe or a star draw ever closer to one another. That is, as a star is about to die, the neutrinos burst forth at light speed, and in the next instant the matter supporting the structure explodes as the star dies, after which a new star is born again from the debris of the old.

In addition, the sun and earth, and even the living creatures on earth, all arise from the debris of stars that exploded and died in the ancient past. Even for humans, who were born in this way, it could well be the phenomenon of that instant when Life and Death merge — imprinted onto our lives — that triggers the homing instinct and the instinct to replicate ourselves, like the salmon that swim upstream, to return to the origin of life, to the birth of the solar system, to the very womb of Creation that stood witness to the birth of the universe.

In the instant the universe was born, there radiated outwardly an infinite sea of Light.

<hr />

Primitive organisms did not die. They simply divided and in this way increased their numbers. But by this process there must have been a huge number of organisms without a simple dead one left behind. As if in answer to Nature's prayer for a better way to manage herself, higher organisms evolved that succumbed to natural death. Higher organisms, however, are complex systems into which death has not been fully integrated, and this has given rise to a number of other attendant phenomena. That is, it may be the very organic complexity of human beings that makes death bring along with it a sense of life being unresolved when they die.

Humans are a complex life form most distant from what Nature herself provides, and perhaps the only way they can negotiate the path going beyond Life and Death, to the point where the two are fully integrated, is through the mediation of the Tathagata. Tathagata is a Sanskrit word meaning "that issuing from Reality-as-Such." Tathata, or Reality-as-Such, being the basic stuff of all things everywhere, the Truth eternal. To have the Tathagata Buddha's mediation as your ally is, in the words of Honen and Shinran, to apply yourself to this Reality "putting your all into the Inconceivable Light."◊

But, even as people today hear about religion and seek to acquire faith, there remains the problem of just how they can grasp this Inconceivable Light as the basic stuff of all things everywhere, as universal Truth. In this connection, Rennyo was a genius at setting these things down in writing. But that was five hundred years ago. Since then, no one has made any effort to get that truth out, and Rennyo's own writings just sit in a nice lacquered box where they are taken out and read on occasion.

People today live putting absolute faith in Life. Death is bad, something to fear and detest, something to rid ourselves of.

Things like funerals are events unrelated to our daily lives. In this sort of age, where talking about death doesn't get through to people, you have to tell them how religion benefits them in their daily lives. But this daily benefit pitch was effective only up to 1965, after which time the GNP and the average life span of Japanese increased, and takers grew increasingly fewer.

Death is what the doctor examines, the dead body is what the mortician looks after, the deceased is what the loved ones looks upon, and "death, the dead body, and the deceased" collectively are what the priest try not to see at all. And as long as the present situation prevails where the priest's income for doing the funeral is all that counts, then there's little we can expect from that quarter of religion. It is only natural that when religion became unable to explain what was going on as it stood in the arena of Life and Death, that it lost its life force and fell from grace.

What's most in demand in every field is to know what's going on when it's going on. It's thus a matter of concern that scholars give precedence to book knowledge of Buddhism. For religion to serve the people living now, religion itself has to be vitally alive. In recent years people have at last noticed that placing value on Life alone is problematic, and as the world enters a period where the elderly in society increase to unprecedented numbers, there's a growing awareness that something has to be done.

Among established religions, greater efforts are being

made to care for the dying. Some programs such as the Vihara movement◊ provide hospices where cancer and AIDS patients can have a better environment to come to terms with death. But for priests who have long lost sight of the goal of coming to terms with death, they have only sermons on weary doctrinal points to fall back on. Visibly flustered as they stand before the dying, they can only come up with trite explanations of Buddhist texts, making a poor show of comforting the person on his deathbed. How useless priests are in this situation is all too apparent.

According to American psychiatrist Dr. Elisabeth Kubler-Ross,◊ who writes from experiences with numerous endstage patients, "The thing that the terminal patient finds the most comforting is to have by his side someone who has by some means overcome death."

That is, the only thing that provides peace of mind to the terminal patient trembling in fear of death is to have someone standing closer to death than he is, all other things being of no account. Gentle words of reassurance, for instance, have no effect, and in many cases may even weigh on the patient more. In other words, having a person like a Bodhisattva at one's side is what works best.

The person the patient can depend on is someone who has had the same experience and who is a little further down the path than he himself is.

There's a pitch-black passage that runs under the main hall

of the Zenkoji◊ temple in Nagano. When you go through there, the best thing is to have someone in front of you so that you can reach out and hold onto someone. Just to have someone ahead of you gives you peace of mind as you move forward. The Buddha has gone too far ahead of us on the path. For Shinran the person who was just a bit ahead of him was his spiritual guide, Honen.

For the endstage patient, encouragement is cruel, reassurance sheer misery, and sermons and talk useless. The only thing they want is a person with eyes like the clear blue sky and who is as transparent as the wind.

> The pampas grass was light, the pebbles in the riverbed
>> shined like crystals, the river flowed like a ribbon of light.
> The trees and the stars and the telephone poles were
>> phosphorescent with flecks of light.
> It's through this world that the Milky Way Express runs.

The scene Kenji Miyazawa describes in *The Night of the Milky Way Express*◊ is little different from that reported by Dr. Imura as he stood in the parking lot of his apartment after he was informed his cancer had spread:

> Everything around me was extremely bright. The people going to the supermarket to shop appeared to be shining. The kids who were running around appeared to be shining. The dogs, the drooping heads of rice, the

weeds, the telephone poles, even down to the tiny pebbles, all appeared to be shining. . . .

This kind of scene, where everything is wrapped in light, is not what the person who is not facing death can see. And, for Shinran, it's all right if you can't see it. Even without seeing it, you should believe in that Inconceivable Light:

> Though people don't come any worse than me,
>> I simply chant the Buddha Name,
> Only to find myself among those swept up
>> into Amida's welcoming arms.
> Afflictions obstruct my eyes
>> to prevent my seeing it,
> Yet Great Compassion never tires
>> as she shines her Light on me.
>
> —FROM *SHOSHINGE*◊

To paraphrase: even those people for whom salvation is impossible are all within the Light. Right now I'm caught in the storm of mental afflictions, and that's the only reason it's impossible for me to see the Light. But the Light of Great Compassion shines on us eternally, and she will continue to shine on us eternally. And so it's good to call the Name of the Buddha.

Whenever I used to do the washing and the coffining, I would have this curious feeling that the corpse I was working on and I were wrapped in an aura. This was also the case when I saw that maggot glow and that light issue from the dragonfly eggs. It brought tears to my eyes.

It's as if we're climbing this long, endless spiral staircase of human desires. When at last it caves in on itself and sends us plummeting in the other direction, as we're falling we catch a glimpse of ourselves in the light as the fragile life form we are. It's like visiting the burned fields of a war-torn land and seeing a single flower blooming. In that moment when Life and Death suddenly integrate, that Inconceivable Light passes before our eyes like a shooting star.

Now I'm living like I used to, dangled about by human desires and selfishness. That light I once saw long out of sight, I'm drowning in love and lust, lost in the search for fame and fortune, living in this dirty world in my own dirty way. That Light remains hidden from sight, as long as there's any trace of human desire or selfishness on our part. "The heart's conversion takes place when you overturn the mind of self-power and dispense with it altogether," says Shinran who tells us it's imperative we rid ourselves of our egos.

In the LifeDeath chapter of *Shobogenzo*, Dogen says,

> Simply do this, step back and, forgetting about that body and mind of yours, take a running dive into the Buddha's house, putting everything you're worth into the hands of the Buddha. When you do just as I've told you, without putting an ounce of physical strength into

it or experiencing any of that unpleasantness that comes with meditation, you pass beyond the struggle between Life and Death and become Buddha.

Thus, in the end we're called upon to rid ourselves of ourselves.

Human desires and selfishness are a frightening thing. How easily trampled underfoot are those worlds of Truth, Good, and Beauty that are the essence of that Inconceivable Light! When an entire tribe is like that, it's even more frightening. When a nation's caught up in selfishness and desires, it becomes war. When a culture's caught up in selfishness and desires, it becomes war. And when a religion's caught up in selfishness and desires, it becomes war. The biggest reason religions go to war is because their leaders still have traces of human selfishness and desires, having never been consecrated by the Light of Reality. Or if a religion's founder was once a person of Reality, his heirs have lost their way in the wilderness of human selfishness and desires.

The Buddha of Light is what brings us to a state brimming with feelings of gratitude toward all living things. Today, people seek that Light among the fruits of the branches of science.

The philosophical tradition from Aristotle to Kant sought a total integration of all branches of human knowledge. But from the nineteenth century to the twentieth century, the branches of science and the twigs of technology went off on their own tangents, and the influence of philosophy and religion grew increasingly less. At present, philosophy has dwindled down to linguistic analysis, while the religionists busy themselves with elucidating the enormous canon inherited from the past.

Inside these developments, science has reached the point where it can say that "the dimension separating subject and object never existed in the first place." There are even scientists who say the boundary of ego vanishes in eternal Life. In 1925, Kenji Miyazawa, in *The Night of the Milky Way Express* writes:

> As everyone knows, water is made up of hydrogen and oxygen. That's something no one would deny. That's because an experiment will prove that it's a fact. But in ancient days there were heated arguments about this, with some saying it was made of mercury and salt and others saying it was made of mercury and sulfur and so on. It was like saying my god is the true god, but even if we believe in different gods altogether, are we not moved to tears by some things that people do? From there we would begin to argue whether our hearts were good or bad. And we would still not come up with a winner. But if you were really to put some study and thought into how to go about the experiment and were able to devise a method to separate out the false ideas, that's where our religious convictions and our scientific beliefs converge.

Thus are the Professor's words to Giovanni, who then invites Giovanni to watch his mysterious experiment:

> Then all of a sudden Giovanni made himself, the ideas he was thinking, the train and the Professor and the Milky Way and everything disappear clean away in a burst of light, and then disappear again in another burst, and again. And in that instant of the flash they could see a vast world spreading out endlessly and all history up to now vanished without a trace and emptied.

After the Professor has verified Giovanni's experiment, he says,

> Well, then, your experiment demands that we bridge the entire strands of disconnected ideas from start to finish. That's the hard part of it.

Through the Professor who appears on the scene, this problem is posed to Giovanni who is an extension of Kenji Miyazawa. Here, Miyazawa brings up the theme of how to integrate the disconnected strands of ideas into oneself.

Science is literally the study of the branches of knowledge, each field being divided into smaller branches. Breaking down the gray areas into smaller sub-branches, Western science can be said to be characterized by this tendency to do research by cutting things up into ever smaller disconnected bits. Ever since the Meiji period in this country, Japanese scholars have loaded up on Western methodology and concentrated all their energy on it. The result is that we find Japanese among the world's leading scientists in many areas. But this kind of disconnected development has gone on unrelated to the quest for human happiness, and has had the unfortunate result of pushing people's hearts into the pit of despair.

Miyazawa feels that the disconnected ideas and assorted things are brought to converge in that single burst of light and for the first time it is possible for them to be integrated.

> As I set forth in life, inspired by what I just experienced, surely I will find the happiness I'm looking for.

So says Giovanni with a ticket to the Bodhisattva path in his hand. To proceed "inspired by what I experienced" alludes to the Bodhisattva. Miyazawa, enamored of *The Lotus Sutra*, is determined to attain the integration, or Reality-as-Such, of the Bodhisattva practices.

If Miyazawa were Shinran, he might have said: "If, in that soft burst of light, you've come to understand that much, simply believe in that Inconceivable Light. For, 'once you've gotten the gist of it, there's no need to read into every little thing the workings of *jinen honisho*.'"

Shinran believed without a doubt that this Inconceivable Light was what the world of Reality-as-Such issued out of. And he placed his faith in this Buddha of Light as existing eternally beyond the rise and fall of the universe, the stars, and all the living creatures on earth. At the same time, he also believed in this Tathagata as a force working to save all living things in mysterious ways.

> I put my entire life into the hands of
> that eternal Life of the
> Tathagata Buddha of Infinite Life,
> I put my life
> into the hands
> of that mysterious Light
> of the Inconceivable Light.

NOTES

Entries are arranged alphabetically. At the end of each note, the page number for the first appearance of the term is indicated. In the text itself, this first occurrence of each term is indicated with a ◊. Unless indicated otherwise, all foreign terms are Japanese.

Afflictions (Jpn. *bonno*, Skt. *klesa*) The so-called passions such as greed, anger and foolishness, that obstruct spiritual progress. In the Path of Spiritual Perfection (*Shodomon*), these afflictions must be eradicated, but in the Path of Pure Land (*Jodomon*) they are affirmed as part of the human condition, only to be transformed into their opposites by the power of Amida's light of compassion. (p. 89)

Altar (*obutsudan*) Found in the homes of many Japanese people. It is where the funeral tablets on which the names of the deceased are inscribed called *ihai*. In popular belief, it is thought to house the souls of the deceased. (p. 52)

Amida Buddha (Skt. *Amitabha*) The Buddha of Infinite Life. The word Amita means the Infinite. The account of Amida Buddha is found in *The Larger Sutra of Infinite Life*. Amida Buddha is also referred to as the Tathagata, the Buddha issuing from Reality-as-Such. (p. 61)

Animism A word that originates in the Greek *anima*, the spirit residing in an object. All forms of belief in a spirit or soul (*reikon*), are called animism. While the spirit cannot be perceived with the physical eye, since ancient times it has been believed to exist. The belief in the existence of the soul is reflected in every society and culture and has strong bearing on how those who live in that sphere think of the world and the life hereafter. In Japan, as the soul, *tamashii*, is thought to depart the body, there is a custom called *tama yobai*, or "soul calling," where one calls the name of the deceased in the direction of the mountains or into the depths of a well. (p. 71)

"The Ballad of Narayama," (*Narayama-bushiko 1957*) A story by Shichiro Fukazawa , (b. 1914). Translated by Donald Keene in 1961 as "The Song of Oak Mountain" in *The Old Woman, The Wife, and The Archer: Three Modern Japanese Short Novels* (New York: Viking Press, 1961). (p. 50)

Become a buddha (*Jobutsu*) Now used as a euphemism to refer to the fact that someone has died. *Jobutsu* originally was a Buddhist technical term meaning to become a buddha, that is, to attain buddhahood as the goal of Buddhist practice. (p. 90)

Birth [in the Pure Land] (*Ojo*) Also used as a euphemism to refer to the fact that someone has died. *Ojo* was originally a Pure Land Buddhist technical term meaning a passage to the Pure Land where Birth into a new Life awaited the seeker. (p. 61)

Brahmanic tradition (*Baramonkyo*) Religion that existed prior to the rise of Buddhism in ancient India that provided the spiritual basis for the caste system. Today, we refer to it as Hinduism. (p. 72)

Buddha (*Butsu*) Can refer to (1) the Buddha as a historical personage such as Shakyamuni, (2) as a suprahistorical principle such as Amida Buddha of the Infinite, or (3) in Japanese, read as "Hotoke-san," refers to a Buddha statue or to the corpse of the deceased. (p. 61)

Chanting the Name of the Buddha Saying the Nembutsu, (*Namu amida-butsu*) as the manifestation of the workings of the Buddha of Infinite Light in one's life. (p. 61)

"Deep in the state of the Great Serenity . . . ," from *Jodowasan*, Pure Land verses in Japanese composed by Shinran. Cf. Hirota. (p. 99)

Dogen (1200-1253) Founder of the Soto school of Zen in Japan. At age three he lost his father and at age eight he lost his mother, impressing upon him the impermanence of life. At age 13 he entered the monastery. He later established the Eihei-ji Zen temple. His *Shobogenzo*, or "Treasury of the True Eye of Reality," had a great influence on later religious philosophers and culture. (p. 103)

"Don't Give in to the Rain," (*Ame ni mo makezu*) One of the poems that Kenji Miyazawa wrote down in his notebook but never published. Cf. Sato, 214. Aoki writes: "There are numerous commentaries on this piece, but to me it conveys well the image of Kenji as a frail poet. It reads: 'Don't give in to the rain, Don't give in to the wind, Don't give in to the snow or summer heat, Keep your body strong.' This is what he wrote while suffering from bouts of unconsciousness at age 35, two years before his death. 'Always keep a serene smile on your face, Four scoops of brown rice a day, Eat this with vegetables and a bit of miso.' This reminds us of Ryokan who lived in a small hut on the temple precincts, eating five scoops of brown rice a day, while smiling and always sitting serenely in his Five Scoop Hut. Ryokan was originally losing 'fights and lawsuits,' and ended up losing everything he had. A true poet gently lives out this desperate *saha* (Skt.) world: 'When the earth became parched, I'd start to shed tears, When summer was unseasonably cold, I'd wander about in a dither, Everyone calling me a useless bump-on-a-log.'" (p. 65)

Einstein, Albert (1879-1955) Physicist who developed the famous theory of relativity. Winner of the 1921 Nobel Prize in physics. Born in Germany, he took asylum in the United States when Nazi persecution of the Jewish people threatened. He was a peace advocate throughout his life. (p. 112)

Eko While this term, meaning "merit transference," is used in general Buddhism to mean that one directs accumulated virtues towards the goal of enlightenment or the liberation of other beings, Shinran interpreted it to mean that Amida Buddha directs his virtues to beings on the path to enlightenment. This is fulfilled in two ways: in order that one can attain birth in the Pure Land, called *oso-eko*, and so that one is empowered to return to the world of delusion to save all beings, called *genso-eko*. (p. 93)

Extending the flower with a smile (*nenge misho*) The legendary episode of the Buddha and Kashyapa, one of his disciples. Only Kashyapa smiled when the Buddha held up a lotus flower before the silent audience at Rajagrha. This transference from mind to mind, symbolized by the lotus flower, is highly regarded in Zen, and is sometimes referred to as the storehouse of the true Dharma eye. (p. 81)

The face radiant with light (*kogen gigi*) The Buddha's radiant countenance described in a well known passage from *The Larger Sutra of Infinite Life*. Ananda is praised by the Buddha for noticing this change that has come over the Buddha and goes on to explain to him the reason for this change. (p. 81)

The February 26th Incident An attempted *coup d'etat* in 1936 by young Japanese army officers that ended in all 19 officers being shot to death by defending guards. It forms the background to Mishima's novel *Yukoku*, 1961. (p. 49)

Five basic elements of earth, water, fire, wind, and space The final element, space, *akasa*, is the place where the physical elements come to full realization. (p. 113)

"The Flames of Persimmon" (*Kaki no hono'o*) A short story by Shinmon Aoki. (p. 13)

For Love of Country (*Yukoku*) 1961, a novel by Yukio Mishima. (p. 49)

Gambatte (Jpn.) Words of encouragement, "Do your best," or "You can do it," such as when a student is about to take a test or take part in a race. When a person is dying, it would mean, "Don't give in until the very end." (p. 53)

Gassho To put one's hands together in reverence. (p. 68)

Genshin (942-1017) Heian Era Tendai monk of high status. He lost his father at a young age and was put into the Tendai monastery on Mount Hiei. His most famous work is known as *Ojoyoshu*, (Essential Passages on Birth). (p. 108)

Hagakure A work on *Bushido* ("the way of the warrior") by Tsunetomo Yamamoto (1659-1719). Several translations of this work are available, among them is: *Hagakure: The Book of the Samurai*, William Scott Wilson, trans. (Kodansha, 1979). (p. 48)

Harakiri To commit suicide by ritual disembowelment. (p. 49)

Hawking, Stephen (b. 1942) Physicist. Graduated from Oxford at the top of his class and matriculated in Cambridge at age 21. Stricken with ALSMND (amyotrophic lateral sclerosis and motor neuron disease) that paralyzed his voluntary muscles and threatened to take his life. Although he is confined to a wheelchair, he continues to be one of the world's leading physicists. His contribution has been to create a link between the theory of relativity and quantum theory, ushering in a new picture of the universe. This universe is one that is completely self-creating, infinite and unbounded, without beginning and without end; it simply exists. Hawking believes that it is possible to postulate this kind of universe on the basis of a completely consistent theory. Now known as TOE. (p. 114)

The Heart Sutra A short Buddhist sutra (scripture) often recited daily by Buddhists of various sects. It is the concise summary of the *Prajnaparamita* or "Perfection of Wisdom." The well known phrase, "Form is emptiness, emptiness is form," comes from this sutra. For a translation from the Sanskrit, see Edward Conze, *Buddhist Wisdom Books: Containing The Diamond Sutra and The Heart Sutra* (London: G. Allen & Unwin, 1966). (p. 65)

Hokuriku The "North Shore" of Japan's main island. (p. 30)

Honen (1133-1212) Founder of the Jodoshu, a school of Pure Land Buddhism. At age eight he experienced the untimely death of his father and soon after entered the monastery. He taught that if one believed in Amida Buddha's vow and said the Nembutsu, they would surely be saved. One of his disciples who faithfully defended the depths of his teaching was Shinran. (p. 79)

Ichimai kishomon (One Sheet Document) Honen's summation of Pure Land teaching. The Bukkyo University homepage version: "Nembutsu is not meditation as taught by the learned men of China and Japan; neither is it recitation through scholarly endeavors in order to master its profound meanings. To realize *Ojo* (birth in the Land of Ultimate Bliss), nothing is required but the implicit faith that the recitation of *Namuamidabutsu* is assurance of *Ojo*. The Three Devotional Hearts and the Four Exercises are encompassed in the firm belief that *Ojo* is assured by the recitation of *Namuamidabutsu*. To expound any thought other than Nembutsu would be contrary to the compassionate mercy of the two venerable buddhas (Shakyamuni Buddha and Amida Buddha) and be in discordance with the Essential Vow of Amida Buddha. One who believes Nembutsu, though he may have learned the entire teachings of Shakyamuni Buddha, should consider himself an illiterate who knows not a single letter and conduct himself as if unschooled as the men and women who shave their heads and observe religious discipline without foundation. Refrain from flaunting knowledge and devote yourself to the recitation of Nembutsu." (p. 79)

"I leave my destiny in your hands" (*Anata makase*) Putting aside one's own efforts and putting one's life in the hands of Amida Buddha. (p. 101)

Impermanence (*Mujo*) The Buddhist truth that all things undergo change and there is no permanent selfhood. (p. 35)

Inconceivable Light (*Fukashigi ko*) One of the characteristics of Amida, the Buddha of Infinite Light. (p. 83)

Intermediate State (Jpn. *chu-u, antarabhava*) a sort of Buddhist purgatory that is actually a part of the world of the living, rather than a separate realm. (p. 69)

Ippen (1239-1289) The founder of Jishu. Exposed to the Tendai teachings from childhood, he entered the monastery at age ten, following the death of his mother. He is well known for spreading *odori* Nembutsu, or dancing Nembutsu, as he wandered throughout the country. For a study and translation, see Dennis Hirota, *The Record of Ippen*

(University of Hawai'i Press, rev. ed. 1999). (p. 108)

Izanagi (Izanagi-no-Mikoto) The god who appears in the Shinto legend of the creation of Japan recorded in the *Kojiki* (*Record of Ancient Matters.*) (p. 28)

Jinen honisho An essay by Shinran in a collection of his letters called *Mattosho.* D. T. Suzuki cites it in his *Mysticism: Christian and Buddhist.* For a recent translation of *Mattosho,* see *The Collected Works of Shinran.* (p. 117)

Jodo Shinshu A school of Pure Land founded by Shinran. It later became a significant force in Japanese society under its eighth hereditary leader Rennyo. One of the largest religious bodies in Japan, the most important of its ten branches is the Nishi Hongwanji with temples in North America, South America and Europe. Also referred to as Shinshu, or Shin Buddhism. (p. 45)

Kaneko, Misuzu (1903-1930) Poet and author of children's books, was born in Yamaguchi prefecture. Praised as a new star in children's poetry, she was a remarkable poet who died at age 26. (p. 104)

Kobayashi, Issa (1763-1827) Poet. Famous haiku poet. Lost all three children and wrote "The World of Dew," after the death of his third child. (p. 100)

Kubler-Ross, Elisabeth (b. 1926) Swiss born psychiatrist, former University of Chicago professor of psychiatric medicine. Her direct experiences with terminal care patients resulted in her best-selling work, *On Death and Dying.* Her other works include *On Children and Death* and *Questions and Answers on Death and Dying.* (p. 123)

Kyogyoshinsho *Teaching, Practice, Realization* Popularly known as, "Teaching, Practice, Faith, Realization," Shinran's main work. (p. 79)

Kyoko's House (*Kyoko no ie*) 1959, a novel by Yukio Mishima. (p. 49)

The Larger Sutra of Infinite Life, (*Daimuryojukyo*) Also known as *The Larger Sutra* an important Mahayana Buddhist sutra on the theme of Amida and the Pure Land. It is regarded as one of the Three Pure Land Sutras, along with *The Smaller Sutra* and *The Meditation Sutra.* (p. 84)

LifeDeath (*Shoji*) Life and death as a unit. The word has been coined to resemble the original Japanese term. For example, the LifeDeath chapter of *Shobogenzo,* by Dogen (*Shobogenzo shoji*) (p. 30)

The Lotus Sutra One of the major Mahayana sutras. For a recent translation, see Burton Watson, trans., *The Lotus Sutra* (New York: Columbia University Press, 1993), based on the Kumarajiva version of the *Saddharmapundarikasutra.*(p. 83)

Mahayana Buddhism (*Daijo Bukkyo*) A popular form of Buddhism based on compassion for all living beings. Aoki writes: "Mahayana means the Large Vehicle, the means by which the larger part of humanity would be able to attain enlightenment. In the centuries after the Buddha's death, lay followers of Buddhism who were located everywhere in India opted to take a direction different from that of the monastic orders. They called themselves Bodhisattvas, or 'seekers of enlightenment.' This term they took from the Jataka stories, the tales of the Buddha's prior lives as he searched for enlightenment. They too were in search of buddhahood, and so they called themselves Bodhisattvas. This movement drew in numerous individuals from the monastic orders, and together with them they created their own unique Mahayana Buddhist literature, consisting of works such as *The Prajnaparamita Sutras, The Lotus Sutra,* the *Vimalakirtinirdesa,* and *The Hua-yen Sutra.*" (p. 82)

Maitreya (*Miroku*) The future Buddha. (p. 118)

Memorial service Services to commemorate the passing of an individual held at regular intervals. *Ho-onko* is a Jodo Shinshu memorial service held to commemorate the death of its founder, Shinran. (p. 46)

The Morning We Parted Forever (*Eiketsu no asa*) A poem by Kenji Miyazawa. Cf. Sato, 83-84. (p. 32)

Mount Hiei A mountain overlooking Kyoto that is the center of the Tendai school. In the medieval period it produced numerous Pure Land thinkers such as Honen and Shinran. (p. 28)

Myoe (1173-1231) An eminent priest of the Kegon school. At age eight he lost his mother, and his father became a war casualty. He entered the monastery at age ten. His most famous work is *Saijarin,* (Destroying Heresy,) a criticism of the principles of Honen's teaching. (p. 108)

Namuamidabutsu The formula for calling the Name of Amida Buddha. Following the classic analysis by T'ang dynasty Pure Land master Shan-tao whose writings inspired Honen. The formula is often understood as the combination of two aspects: the *Namu* of the seeker and the *Amidabutsu* of the Buddha. These two aspects come together in the recitation of the formula *Namuamidabutsu.* (p. 92)

Namandabu An abbreviated orally recited form of *Namuamidabutsu.* (p. 32)

Name of the Buddha *Namuamida-butsu* is the Name (*myogo*) that contains the forty-eight vows of Amida Buddha. When one invokes the Name and is awakened to its significance, one receives immeasurable benefits (p. 61)

Nembutsu The recitation of the formula "*Namuamidabutsu,*" the critical act that decides one's Birth in the Pure Land. The practice of Nembutsu goes beyond the Pure Land and is found in early Chinese Tendai and Zen practice as well. In the Tendai practice of the constantly walking *samadhi,* the seeker circumambulates the statue of a Buddha for periods of up to one hundred days, while constantly reciting the Name of the Buddha. Chinese Zen practice also incorporated Nembutsu recitation. In Japan, Honen devoted himself to long sessions of Nembutsu practice, counting with his beads the tens of thousands of times he recited the formula within the space of a day. One purpose of such practice was to enter the state of Nembutsu *samadhi,* a trancelike state in which the world becomes transparent. (p. 96)

The Night of the Milky Way Express (*Ginga tetsudo no yoru*) A story by Kenji Miyazawa. Aoki writes: "The extracts I have cited are compiled from two different editions of Miyazawa's collected works, Shunpei Kusano's *Miyazawa Kenji* and Chikuma's *Miyazawa Kenji Zenshu*. Miyazawa reworked this material numerous times, especially the closing portion where he relates the fourth dimension." (p.124)

Ojuzu Also called Onenju or Mala. The Ojuzu is a string of beads used in Buddhist rituals and meditation. In Jodo Shinshu, it is draped over the hands, under the thumbs, when one puts his hands together in gassho. The Catholic rosary and Muslim worry beads are believed to have been derived from the Ojuzu. (p. 3)

Path of Self-Perfection (*Shodomon*) In contrast to *Jodomon*, or the Path of the Pure Land. In the latter, one believes in Amida Buddha's promise and after dying is welcomed to the Pure Land where one attains enlightenment. In the former, one trusts in one's own innate ability to complete practices and to attain enlightenment in this world. This distinction was first established by the Chinese Pure Land thinker Tao-ch'o who set up various categories with which to view the Buddhist teachings in his *An-lo chi* (Collection of Verses on Peace and Happiness.) (p. 97)

The person who is sure to attain buddhahood (*Shojoju*) Literally, "properly determined rank," the person who is sure to attain nirvana. Since one's buddhahood is guaranteed, this is the same as being a buddha-in-the-making. (p. 96)

Pope Pius XII As cited in Dr. John A. O'Keefe, in Robert Jastrow, God and the Astronomers [New York, London: W. W. Norton, 1978; second edition, 1992], p. 120 (p. 113)

(Skt.) **Pratityasamutpada** (*Innen*) The interdependence of all living things. (p. 116)

Pure Land The realm created by Amida Buddha out of his efforts to make a land to receive all beings who call his Name. Also used to refer to the school of Buddhism of that name. See Pure Land 2 (p. 61)

Pure Land (*Jodo*) A popular form of Mahayana Buddhism with roots in India that developed especially in China and Japan. Its early adherents believed in Birth in a Pure realm in the western direction, based on the sutras describing the *buddhaksetra*, or "buddha realm," of Amitabha, the Buddha of Infinite Light. The writings of Chinese Pure Land masters such as T'an-luan, Tao-ch'o, and Shan-tao later inspired Kamakura Pure Land teachers such as Honen and Shinran. In Japan, Pure Land Buddhism had a strong appeal for ordinary people in the agrarian-based society of medieval and premodern times. (p. 61)

Putting your all into the Inconceivable Light (*Namu fukashikigo*) A free translation for an alternate formula of reciting the Buddha Name. (p. 121)

Record of Ancient Matters (*Kojiki*) An early translation is Basil Hall

Chamberlain, *Kojiki,* or *Records of Ancient Matters* (Tokyo: Asiatic Society of Japan, 1906). (p.28)

Rennyo (1415-1499) Eighth hereditary leader descending from Shinran of the Hongwanji lineage of the Jodo Shinshu. He was separated from his mother at the age of six when his father was obliged to marry a woman of standing, which his mother was not. Overcoming many difficulties, he went on to make an insignificant lineage, the Hongwanji, into a national institution. For a booklength study and translation, see Rogers & Rogers, *Rennyo* (1992). Alfred Bloom also has essays devoted to Rennyo on www.shindharmanet.com on the internet. (p. 108)

Rimbaud, Arthur (1854-1891) Poet. He wrote poems from ages 15 to 19 and wrote the famous poem "The Drunken Boat" at age 17. When he died at 37, he was a merchant who had traveled all over the world. (p. 101)

Schrödinger, Erwin (1887-1961) German physicist, the father of quantum physics. In 1933 he was awarded the Nobel Prize in physics for "the discovery of new productive forms of atomic theory," which is the title of his presentation speech at the ceremony. (p. 113)

Sermon Ballad (*Sekkyo bushi*) A genre of medieval tales related by a story-teller. It originated in sermons on Buddhist teachings made by wandering priests on street corners known as *kado-sekkyo* or "corner sermons." As it developed to include poetry and songs, in time it became popular as performances with musical instruments such as *kokyu* and *shamisen.* It is also called *sekkyo joruri,* often comical skits with a Buddhist theme and a moral twist. (p. 51)

Shakyamuni The historical founder of Buddhism. (p. 62)

Shinran (1173-1262) Founder of the Jodo Shinshu school. He was separated from his mother at the age of eight. At age 28, he left the monastic life on Mount Hiei and joined the Pure Land community begun by Honen (1133-1212). He was exiled to a rural area where he built up a following. For his works, see *The Collected Works of Shinran.* (1997) (p. 61)

Shinran the Foolish and Stubble-headed (*Gutoku Shinran*) A name that Shinran chose for himself as a declaration of his independence indicating that he was neither a monk or a lay person. For his writings, see *The Collected Works of Shinran.* (1997) (p. 102)

Shinto A native Japanese religion. Adherents believe that all things, such as trees and stones and grasses, contain spirits. (p. 28)

Shoshinge (*Song of Faith*) Buddhist verses about the transmission of the Pure Land Teachings from India to China to Japan composed by Shinran. (p. 125)

Six realms (*rokudo*) The Buddhist notion that living things are in an endless cycle of birth and rebirth, in the six realms of *devas* (Skt., heavenly beings), humans, *ashuras* (Skt., warring spirits), beasts, *pretas* (Skt., hungry ghosts) and hells. (p. 69)

"Spring and Ashura" (*Haru to ashura*) A poem by Kenji Miyazawa. (p. 83)

Tathagata (Skt. *Nyorai*) That issued from Reality-as-Such. (p. 83)

Tathagata Buddha The Buddha issuing from Reality-as-Such. (p. 84)

Tathata (*Shinnyo*) Literally, "true suchness," Reality-as-Such (p. 112)

Tannisho "Grievous Differences" A treatise by Yui-en written some time after Shinran's death in 1263. It includes the sayings of Shinran, as recalled by the author, and attempts to correct deviations of the teachings that were current. Rennyo, the eighth hereditary leader of the Hongwangji lineage regarded the contents open to misunderstanding, so he advised that it not be shown to outsiders. In the twentieth century it became a major work for understanding Shin Buddhism, and it remains one of the most popular works on Pure Land Buddhism in contemporary Japan. It deals with the human potential on both the conscious and unconscious levels. What we think are good and evil on the conscious level fails to realize that our karmic past contained in the unconscious ultimately determines our actions. For recent translation, see *The Collected Works of Shinran*. (p. 61)

"Telling It with My Eyes," (*Me ni te iu*) A poem by Kenji Miyazawa. (p. 67)

Ten Kings A sutra that was popular in China that told of the departed soul's appearance before Yama, King of the Underworld in the afterlife. It is thought to be an amalgamation of Chinese folk beliefs and Buddhist thought. Along with the memorial services to direct merit to the deceased on the 49th day, the 100th day, the first year, and so on, it became very popular. (p. 94)

Toyama A prefecture in the Hokuriku or "North Shore" area of Japan's main island. It is surrounded by the Tateyama mountain range that provides it with the fresh water for which Toyama is famous. Toyama is also one of the strongholds of Jodo Shinshu in the Hokuriku area and is closely connected with many developments in its history. (p. 6)

Transmigration (*rinne*) An ancient Indian notion that Buddhism interpreted to mean that one is reborn into an endless cycle of suffering. (p. 112)

Triple world The worlds of desire, form and nonform. (Skt. *raga, rupa, arupa*) (p. 115)

Unimpeded Light Group (*Mugeko-shu* or *Mugeko-ryu*) A popular Pure Land group during Rennyo's time that was criticized and persecuted by the Mount Hiei monastics. It took its name from "Kimyo Jinjippo Mugeko Nyorai," one of the recitations for the Buddha of Infinite Light. (p. 96)

Vihara movement The word *vihara* is a Sanskrit term meaning a safe dwelling place, comfort, a monk's lodging. The term Vihara has been used in connection with the hospice movement in Japan, based on a Buddhist form of caring. (p. 123)

Wasan (literally, "verses in Japanese") Verses in praise of Buddha, Bodhisattvas, eminent teachers and predecessors, these *wasan* were

Buddhist form of caring. (p. 123)

Wasan (literally, "verses in Japanese") Verses in praise of Buddha, Bodhisattvas, eminent teachers and predecessors, these *wasan* were later overlaid onto Buddhist chants during the Edo period, 1603-1868. In addition to Shinran's the famous *wasan* include Genshin's praises of the Pure Land and elegies on the Buddha's appearance at one's deathbed. (p. 51)

"White Ashes" (*Hakkotsu no sho*) A letter by Rennyo. The title alludes to a passage that goes, "Though in the morning we may have radiant health, in the evening we may be white ashes," (p. 31)

"The Winter River" (*Sai no kawara*) A medieval tale of a little boy who dies and crosses the winter river. He tries to build a small stupa for the repose of his parents' souls, but every time he builds one, demons come along and knock it down, until he is rescued by Jizo Bodhisattva. This forms part of the basis of Jizo worship popular throughout Japan and the local Jizo festivals for children held in the summer in Kyoto. (p. 51)

Zen The school of meditation that flourished in China, Korea and Japan. (p. 81)

Zenkoji An ancient Buddhist temple in Nagano prefecture, once a site on the pilgrimage route that all people ideally undertook once in their lifetime. (p. 124)

BIBLIOGRAPHY

Aoki, Shinmon *Nokanfu nikki* ["Coffinman Diary"] (Tokyo: Bungei Shunju, rev. ed. 1996).

Imura, Kazukiyo *Arigato, minasan* ("Thank you everyone"), later republished under the title "*Asuka e, soshite mada minu ko e*" [To Asuka, and to the child whom I've yet to meet] (Shoden-sha.)

Jastrow, Robert "God and the astronomers" (New York : W. W. Norton, 1978; rev. ed. 1992).

Kaneko, Misuzu *Kaneko Misuzu zenshu*, Vol. I (JULA Shuppankyoku).

Rennyo "White Ashes" *Hakkotsu no sho*, Taitetsu Unno, trans., unpublished,

Miyazawa Kenji "A future of ice: Poems and stories of a Japanese Buddhist," Hiroaki Sato, trans. (San Francisco: North Point Press, 1989).

Shinran *The Collected Works of Shinran*, two volumes (Kyoto: Nishi Hongwanji, 1997). A translation of all of Shinran's writings.

Suzuki, Ayako "*Gan kokuchi no ato de: Watashi no Nyozegamon*" (After I was told I had cancer: My experiencing of hearing the truth [that Buddhism teaches] with my own ears) (Tankyusha 1989)

Takami, Jun "*Shi no fuchi yori*" (From the brink of death) (1964; Kodansha, 1971).

COFFINMAN ORDER FORM

Online orders:	amazon.com or becbooks.com
Telephone orders:	800-247-6553
Postal orders:	Please send this form to: BookMasters PO Box 388 Ashland, Ohio 44805

Name _____

Address _____

City _____ State _____ Zip _____

Email address _____

Telephone number _____

Price:	Books are $14.95 each
Sales tax:	Please add 7.75% for books shipped to California. Ohio residents add 6.25%
Shipping:	US $3.95 for the first book and $1.45 for each additional book. Please call for international shipping orders
Payments:	Money orders and checks made payable to BookMasters

Qty.	Price	Total
	$14.95	
Tax if applicable CA 7.75% OH 6.25%		
Shipping and Handling		
Total Enclosed		

BUDDHIST EDUCATION CENTER

bca-ocbc.org